Contents

Acknowledgements

The publisher would like to thank the following people for supplying the photographs in this book:

Aycliff and Peterlee Development Corporation 108 right; Birmingham Post & Mail 136; Jane Bown/The Observer 141; John Bright & Bros. Ltd 108 left; Fiona Corbridge 13 bottom right; County Joinery, Petworth 132; Cull Photographic 137; Chris Honeywell, Honeywell Information Systems/Gold Greenlees Trott 176 bottom; Mail Newspapers plc 134; National Graphical Association 142; Polygram/Burson-Marsteller 131; Rowntree Mackintosh/J. Walter Thompson 176 top; Texas Instruments 89; Thorn-EMI 130; Andrew Wiard/Report 127; WINIT (W. Little & Sons Ltd.) 193.

The publisher is grateful to the following for permission to reprint textual material: The County of Avon 9; Derbyshire County Council 20; Northern Foods 34; The Boots Company plc 35; Britoil 37; The National Westminster Bank 40–41; Nottinghamshire County Council 43; Netherton Ales plc 51; Saatchi and Saatchi Compton Ltd 86; IBM United Kingdom Ltd 93; Hugh Marshall 139; Footloose 193 (top), Climber and Rambler 193 (bottom).

THE ORGANIZATION IN ITS ENVIRONMENT

1

Stephanie Howkins

Trent Polytechnic

General Editors
John Eve
North Staffordshire Polytechnic
Allister Langlois
Guernsey College of Further Education

Oxford University Press 1987

Oxford University Press,
Walton Street, Oxford OX2 6DP

Oxford New York Toronto
Delhi Bombay Calcutta Madras Karachi
Petaling Jaya Singapore Hong Kong Tokyo
Nairobi Dar es Salaam Cape Town
Melbourne Auckland

and associated companies in
Beirut Berlin Ibadan Nicosia

© Stephanie Howkins 1987
Oxford is a trade mark of Oxford University Press

ISBN 019 833531 8

Typeset by MS Filmsetting Limited, Frome,
Somerset

Printed in Great Britain by The Alden Press Ltd., Oxford.

The Organization in its Environment 1

OR 29.9.93

Coverage of Indicative Content of BTEC Unit
The Organization in its Environment 1

Block 1
Personnel, Employment and the Individual
The individual and the
  organization
Personnel policies
Manpower planning
Resource mix
Types and levels of policy
Education and training

Block 2
Organizations and the Private Sector
Classification of
  organizations
Choice between business
  units
Public/private sector
  interface
Raising of finance
Purposes and use of finance
Organizational structures
Competition and planning

Block 3
Organizations and the Public Sector
Classification of
  organizations
Organizational structures
Resource mix
Scale of operations
Raising of finance
Purposes and uses of finance

Block 4
Objectives and Policies
Types of business objectives
Types and levels of policy
Causes of change
The relevance of technology
Scale of operations
Identification of information
  needs
Purposes of information
Structural changes (internal
  to an organization)

Block 5
Organizations and Decisions
Organizational structures
Causes of change
Decision-making processes
Purposes of information
Constraints

Block 6
Organizations and Employment Legislation; Changing Life at Work
Causes of change
Employment law
Industrial and human
  relations
Termination of employment
Constraints
Political and legal change

Block 7

Production, Technology and Change

Causes of change
Differing responses to change
Technical changes
Changes in employment
　needs
Development of processes
The relevance of technology
Nature of the technology
Functions of the processes
Cost implications
De-skilling and retraining
Conflict resolution
Resource mix
Resource scarcity and
　profitability
Industrial and human
　relations
Technical and economic
　efficiency
Constraints

Block 8

Marketing: The Customer is King

Organizational structures
Causes of change
Changes in market sector
　and marketing strategy
Scale of operations
Identification of information
　needs
Sources of information
Market types
Competition and monopoly
Marketing mix
Determinants of demand
Demand and supply in price
　determination

Block 9

Case Study: A Firm Wrongfooted by the Pace of Change

Causes of change
Responses to change
Technical changes
Changes in employment
　needs
Cost implications
Organizational impact
De-skilling and retraining
Changes in market sector
Termination of employment
Conflict resolution
Resource mix
Identification of information
　needs
Industrial and human
　relations
Technical and economic
　efficiency
Termination of employment
Constraints

Introduction

Approach and method

It is important to study this intro- duction before making use of the book This book has been written mainly for students studying for a Business and Technician Education Council (BTEC) National Level award which includes the unit, *The Organization in its Environment 1*. The BTEC award stresses the need to develop skills while studying, and hence regards study as a very active process. Simply acquiring knowledge is not enough in itself and so skills in the application of that knowledge must be developed if the award is to be really useful to the student.

A traditional textbook which simply outlines the facts which are part of the syllabus is therefore not likely to satisfy the needs of a BTEC student. Such a traditional approach centres its attention on the author's or teacher's knowledge and their choice of how to present it. The BTEC approach centres on the individual needs of the reader or student and seeks to involve them actively in the learning process.

This book provides a series of learning activities which should stimulate the reader to be involved in the learning process in an active manner. The reader is required to participate in the acquisition of locally relevant and up-to-date knowledge and the activities provided should develop the reader's skills in applying that knowledge.

Each block in this book examines aspects of organizations and the interaction between them and their environment. The activities suggested are designed to develop knowledge and skills relevant to the unit, and guidance is also provided on specific organizational knowledge which might be required for the completion of the activities.

It is intended that students and lecturers will be able to make use of all the blocks contained within the book to achieve coverage of the unit. Alternatively, individual blocks of work may be selected and used independently or in conjunction with the lecturer's own material. The activities are not intended to be used in their present form as BTEC assignments but some of them may be suitably adapted for that purpose. Neither is it necessary for the student to complete every single activity in the book in order to study the course successfully. In some cases it may be more appropriate to think briefly about the activity and then, having studied the guidance section, to proceed to the next activity. If you are a student on a full-time course you would be well advised to attempt as many of the activities as possible, since you should have time for studying and will not have had experience of the subject matter at work. If you are a part-time student, your time for studying will probably be more limited so you should select those activities from which you will learn most.

It is important to recognize that there are no 'right answers' to most of the set activities, and that in some cases the 'answer' consists of encouraging you to ask appropriate further questions. In addition to this the activities will require you to make use of skills, and to a more limited extent knowledge, developed in the *Finance* and *People in Organizations* units.

Summary of how to use this book

1 Select a block to study. There is logical development in the organization of the blocks, but if your course is working in a different sequence then there is no reason why you should not change the order.

2 Work through the activities alone or together with colleagues on your course. If you need guidance on any particular aspect of the activity, you should find useful information following the activity. Remember also that the index should help you to find information you require.

3 If you find any aspect of the work puzzling, then be sure to ask for help from your lecturer or teacher, or, if appropriate, consult somebody at work.

Block 1
Personnel, Employment and the Individual

Introduction

Most people will spend a large proportion of their life at work. Indeed, out of all the organizations with which we come into contact, it is our work organization which we know best. The first contact which most people make with their work organization is usually in response to an advertisement for personnel.

The learning activities in this block are designed to help you consider the process of managing people at work. The activities which you will be involved in will draw on your own experience either as employees or potential employees, but will also require an understanding of the functions of personnel management, particularly those linked to the acquisition of employees.

| *Activity 1* | If you are a part-time student then you can use your own job for this task. |

If you are studying full-time then you will need to carry out some preliminary research. Simply do what you would have to do if you were looking for a full-time, permanent job. Make use of your local Job Centre and newspapers to find out what sort of jobs are available for you, and select one.

Write a job description for your chosen job. This should give details of the post and provide a brief introduction to the organization. The information should be suitable to send out to applicants.

Before an organization recruits a person some thought must be given to the job which is to be advertised and the type of person who will be required to fill it.

The job description

A job description should say what is involved in a job. It is a statement of the general purpose of the job, which also provides an outline of its scope, duties, and responsibilities. The sort of detail which would need to be included to describe a job would be:

1 the job title and the name of the department in which the job is located,
2 the tasks involved in the job itself,
3 its position within the organization, ie what the job holder is responsible for and to whom he reports,
4 the objectives which should be achieved,
5 the hours of work and location.

No job description can be expected to be comprehensive in terms of every minute detail of the job, but it should give sufficient information to:

1 give the job holder a clear picture of what is expected in the job;
2 give some indication of the level of the job and the responsibility involved;
3 identify the important or critical areas of the job;
4 provide a full and accurate reflection of work required in order to aid the development of suitable training programmes.

In some organizations job descriptions may be obtained through the process of job analysis, ie the systematic study of all the facts about a job. This is usually carried out by a trained job analyst. In other organizations, line managers may be responsible for drawing up job descriptions for their own members of staff.

If the description is drawn up by a job analyst then it is usual for the analyst to write up the job description in a standard format, in conjunction with the job holder and the job holder's superior. Where there are a number of people doing the same job, the analyst will agree the description with a representative of the group, who will often be the trade union representative or staff representative for the employees concerned.

Some organizations may choose not to draw up job descriptions but to leave the scope of the job to the individual. One argument used in favour of this approach is that if people with initiative are appointed then they should not be limited in their work by being required to adhere to precise terms of reference. In addition, it is suggested that in most organizations conditions are constantly changing and therefore responsibilities attached to a particular job become out of date very quickly. Advocates of the use of job descriptions would argue that the definition of responsibilities is essential if management is to ensure that no area of work is overlooked because nobody has clear responsibility for doing it.

To be useful, job descriptions need to be full and accurate reflections of work done and a key task for personnel specialists and management is to ensure that job descriptions are regularly updated. An example of a job description is given below.

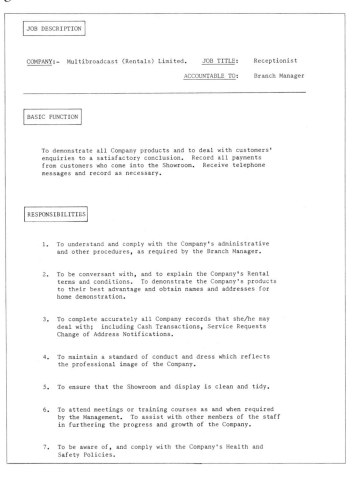

A job description.

Job specifications

A job specification is a detailed statement of the skills and knowledge required by any holder of the job. It indicates what the management feel is required of any person in order for the job to be performed adequately. Clearly, what is written in the job specification in terms of the qualifications and experience necessary must be justified by reference to the duties and responsibilities noted in the job description.

Below is an example of a job specification, which details both skills and knowledge required to do the job, but which also details duties and responsibilities. In practice therefore organizations may not separate the functions of a job description and a job specification.

COUNTY OF AVON
JOB SPECIFICATION

DEPARTMENT	DIVISION OR SECTION	
Chief Executive	Computer Development Unit	

JOB TITLE	POST No.	GRADE
Systems Analyst (Project Leader)	CCE/CDU/13002/13003 13004/13006/13007/00409	PO(1)

JOB PURPOSE:

1. Under the direction of the Senior Systems Analyst (Group Leader), to analyse departmental information processing requirements and to investigate and implement hardware and/or software, including any necessary design of software to meet those requirements.

DUTIES AND RESPONSIBILITIES:

2. (a) To determine, in accordance with terms of reference, the requirements for information processing systems and to participate in feasibility studies for major developments.

   (b) To define work volumes and frequency of processes so that operating facilities and costs can be estimated and to prepare documentation as a basis for agreement with users.

   (c) To develop new systems by preparing:-

      (i) Specifications

      (ii) Form designs and report layouts.

      (iii) Operating instructions for data preparation or input, computing and output handling equipment.

      (iv) Plans and instructions for the transfer of records to the new system.

      (v) Systems test data and results.

   (d) To specify equipment and staff requirements for the operation of the proposed systems.

   (e) To work with user staff, or officers of the Management Services Division on areas of systems development related to clerical and mechanical procedures.

   (f) To assist and to help provide user departments with the appropriate training, file conversion, trial running and consolidation entailed in introducing new systems and to help develop expertise in the hardware, software and communication tools supported.

   (g) To assist in the evaluation of information processing equipment, networks and software and to investigate current developments in computing hardware, software and communications in order to assess their potential impact on Avon's long term strategy for computing.

   (h) To help develop a purchasing policy for computing hardware, software and communications equipment, and to identify suitable tools upon which the Authority may standardise and which can be made available to departments within the corporate strategy.

   (i) To assist in providing the means to the users enabling them to make use of information held on mainframe or minicomputers used by the Authority.

   (j) To assist in the promotion of computing, new technology, information processing and related techniques and to provide users with a general consultancy service and help them with any computing problems they may have.

   (k) To compile reports for management and Committees as necessary and to represent a Senior Systems Analyst at Committee and other meetings.

(Continue on separate plain A4 sheet if necessary)

Extract from a job specification

| Activity 2 | Assuming that you were actually applying for the job which you have described in Activity 1, make a list of all the things you would want to know about it. |

Much of the information which you would want to know about a job must in fact be included in a **contract of employment.** The list which you have compiled for Activity 2 is likely to be quite wide ranging, and will probably have included the following:

1 details of pay, including pay structure and whether there are annual increments or a bonus,
2 details of staff facilities, eg discount on goods, overalls, a canteen,
3 hours of work,
4 holiday entitlement, eg whether it increases with service,
5 training, eg whether it is provided by the company or whether there are facilities for day release,
6 promotion prospects,
7 general conditions of work.

Your list may differ to some degree from this one, but it is likely that many of the items which you have suggested are those which must be included in a contract of employment.

The contract of employment

As soon as a person agrees to work for an employer and the employer agrees to pay wages, then a contract exists. The Employment Protection Consolidation Act 1978 requires an employer to give all employees over the age of 18, working for sixteen or more hours a week, written details of the terms of the contract of employment.

The written statement is not a contract of employment in itself: once the employer makes an offer of employment to an individual and this is accepted, a contract is in existence. This need not take the form of a written document, though it is customary for it to do so. The details of the contract are known as the terms and conditions, and an employer must give each employee a written statement setting out the main particulars of the employment within thirteen weeks of the date of engagement.

The object of the written statement is to give employees a clear understanding of their rights and obligations under their contract of employment and it must cover the following points:

1 title and grade of job,
2 the date when employment began,
3 the minimum period of notice of termination of employment required by both parties (this will depend upon length of service),
4 the rate of pay and methods of calculating it,
5 the interval at which earnings are to be paid, ie weekly, monthly,
6 hours of work and holiday entitlement,
7 details of payment when away from work through illness (sick pay),
8 details of pension scheme provision,
9 details of the procedure if a grievance arises,
10 details of the organization's disciplinary rules.

It would be helpful if you could look at your own contract of employment or, if you are not working, at someone else's. You will then get an idea of how the written particulars are expressed.

You may find that some items are not detailed fully but reference is made to a document which gives the information. Such a document is often a collective agreement which has been negotiated by the trade union responsible for the employees and agreed with the employer. Employees must however be able to obtain access to the document.

If an employee does not receive written details within the thirteen week time limit, or if the document is thought to be incorrect, then an employee can take the matter to an industrial tribunal. The tribunal has the power to make an order that the employer should supply written particulars.

Opposite is a standard form for a contract of employment. Note the layout and the detail covered.

Activity 3

Using the standard form shown opposite for the contract of employment and the details of the job used for Activity 1, draw up a contract of employment for the job.

Twinlock
Business Forms

Employee to be given top copy   Employer to retain duplicate

THIS FORM IS DESIGNED TO ASSIST EMPLOYERS IN MEETING THE REQUIREMENTS OF THE EMPLOYMENT PROTECTION (CONSOLIDATION) ACT 1978.

Employment Protection (Consolidation) Act 1978

This statement dated _____ sets out the main particulars of the terms and conditions on which:

[NAME OF EMPLOYER] _____ employs [NAME OF EMPLOYEE] _____

✳ Your employment began on _____ and employment with your previous employer does not count as part of your continuous period of employment

✳ Your employment began on _____ and as your previous employment with _____ counts as part of your continuous period of employment this is deemed to have begun on _____

✳ Delete where applicable

Part 1 – Main Terms and Conditions

Title of job	You are employed as:
Pay	Your salary/wage will be paid at intervals by cash/cheque/banker's order. Details:
Normal hours of work	Your normal hours are: Other terms and conditions:
Holiday entitlement and pay	
Sickness or injury	Details of terms and conditions and any sick pay benefits (if none, say so)
Pensions and pension schemes	Schemes in operation (if none, say so)
Rights to notice Termination of Employment	Notice to be given by employer: Notice to be given by employee: By mutual agreement these notices can be waived by either party. Payment in lieu of notice may be accepted.
Fixed contracts	If service is by fixed contract no period of notice should be given but date of expiry of fixed term is entered here

Part 2 – Additional Note

Disciplinary rules	State any disciplinary rules applicable to the employee (or refer to any document that contains any disciplinary rules)
	If you are dissatisfied with any disciplinary decision you should raise it orally/in writing with:
Grievance procedure	If you have any grievance relating to your employment you should raise it orally/in writing with:
Social security pensions	A contracting out certificate is/is not in force for the employment in respect of which this statement is given.

© Twinlock   Any changes of terms mentioned above will be notified within one month, and the office record is available for inspection   To re-order quote E55

A contract of employment.

Recruitment and selection

Recruitment and selection are parts of the process by which organizations obtain new employees from the external labour market. This process will include the preparation of job descriptions and specifications, defining the nature of the job and the skills and qualifications required for the job, the selection of the appropriate media for advertising the post, and the processing of applications.

It is vital to attract candidates with the necessary qualifications and the right sort of experience for the job. If the advertising of the post fails to do this, then the subsequent selection procedure may well be a waste of time or effort, with either the wrong person being appointed or the organization failing to appoint at all.

Activity 4	Obtain a copy of your local newspaper and examine the *situations vacant* pages.

a Make a list of the sorts of jobs advertised.
b What sort of information is provided to prospective job applicants?
c Are there any jobs advertised which are not locally based?

It is important to advertise in the correct place, whether that may be a local newspaper, national newspaper, specialist journal or some other outlet. It is also important to ensure that the content of the advertisement is accurate with regard to the nature of the work to be done and the experience and qualifications required. In addition it is important to ensure that the advertisement complies with various legal requirements governing recruitment advertising.

Parts of the Sex Discrimination Act 1975 and the Race Relations Act 1976 are relevant to recruitment and provide job applicants with protection from discrimination by employers on grounds of sex, marital status, race, colour, nationality or ethnic or national origin.

Perhaps one of the most obvious effects of the Sex Discrimination Act has been in the field of recruitment advertising. The legislation requires that there should be nothing in the wording of advertisements to suggest that jobs are open to some groups and not to others.

Apart from advertising in the press, employers may fill vacancies from various private and public employment agencies. Local Job Centres carry details of many local employment opportunities and private employment bureaux and agencies help to put organizations in touch with suitable job applicants. In larger organizations personnel departments will also maintain contact with other potential sources of recruits, eg colleges and universities.

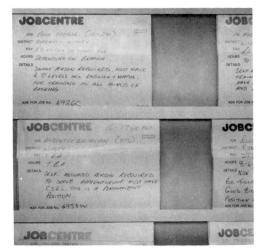

A Job Centre, and Job Centre advertisements.

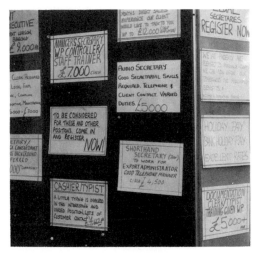

A private employment agency and job advertisements.

Internal appointments

The internal appointment of employees to vacancies within an organization may offer a number of benefits. The promotion of an employee who is known to be capable and reliable and is familiar with the organization may provide greater certainty than appointing someone from outside. In addition the knowledge that internal promotions are possible may well motivate employees, whereas consistent appointments from outside the organization may suggest that there are few prospects for those already working within the organization.

Selection

The selection process which is carried out by organizations to find the right person for a particular job may vary in length but, if the source is the external labour market, then it will invariably involve the use of an application form.

| *Activity 5* | Also using the job for which you have produced a job description in Activity 1, draw up a suitable application form for the job. You will need to decide what information you would require from an applicant. Take care over the design and layout of the form.

When you have prepared the form, check your information requirements with those given below.

One of the functions of an application form is to provide information about the candidates for a job, for example,
1 personal details: name, address, date of birth, etc,
2 educational experience and qualifications,
3 details of past work experience and jobs,
4 personal interests,
5 suitability for the job.

You may find it useful to obtain copies of application forms to make a comparison of the details requested. You could obtain examples easily by looking at the job advertisements in your local newspaper, and telephoning two or three organizations for application forms.

It is unlikely that the application form will be the only device used for selecting an employee. Normally the information provided is used as a screening device to identify unsuitable candidates. The main aim of an organization will be to follow a selection process, of which the application form is just a part, leading to the appointment of a suitable employee.

| *Activity 6* | Think about the process involved within an organization from the receipt of completed application forms, to the appointment of the selected applicant. Draw a simple flow chart showing the main stages of the selection process, beginning with the receipt of applications and ending with the appointment. Use the same job as for earlier activities in this block. Try to think of any particular problems or considerations.

There will of course be variations in the selection process used, depending upon the organization and the post involved. Compare your flow chart for Activity 6 with the one given below; make sure that the process which you have suggested is logical.

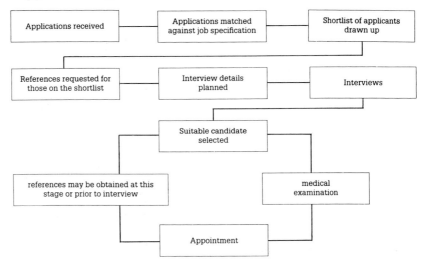

Flow chart for the selection process.

The personnel function

Within organizations it is the Personnel Department which will be responsible for recruitment and selection in liaison with the appropriate departmental manager. The function of a personnel department is to assist with the acquisition, development and retention of the human resources necessary for the success of an organization. Specific responsibilities might include:

1 recruiting and selecting employees,
2 training and development of employees to fit them for their work,
3 appraising the performance of certain employees in order to obtain more effective working,
4 administering wage and salary systems,
5 involvement in industrial relations, negotiations with trade unions, guidance on employment legislation,
6 provision of welfare and counselling services to employees.

In order to ensure that there is effective management of an organization's employees it is necessary to formulate personnel policies, ie guidelines for action, and to oversee their implementation.

Personnel problems and policies

In order to examine the diversity of activities involved in personnel work we will look at a number of personnel problems which could arise and examine the policies which could be pursued in order to solve them.

Read the case study which follows. It gives details of a firm which is facing a number of personnel problems.

T.K. Engineering

T.K. Engineering is a small, well-established company based in the West Midlands. It produces components specifically for domestic car manufacturers including British Leyland. They have managed to stay in business despite the recession, but only by maintaining their competitiveness through heavy investment in new technology.

The workforce of seventy-five comprises fifteen administrative/office staff and sixty production workers. Sixty per cent of the production workers are women.

Over the last two years the entire production process has been automated, virtually eliminating all manual production methods. The move towards automated production should mean a substantial improvement in the firm's profitability. It has had major repercussions for manning levels and all of the production workers have had to become familiar with the new working methods. Because of this, the Production Manager decided to allocate workers to specific points on the production process and to leave them on that work. When asked if he would consider allowing people to move around the production line, he said that such a policy would defeat the whole point of installing the new automated process. The idea was that each individual should become highly skilled at their particular task.

On a number of occasions over the last six months the daily production target has not been met. An increasing number of the production workers have been absent from work for odd days, or arriving late in the morning, which causes hold-ups on the production line. All production workers clock on, and if late they lose half an hour's pay. This means that although they may only be five minutes late, half an hour's pay is deducted.

The Production Manager is also aware that some of his best production operatives have recently left the company to join a rival components firm which has just won a large contract from a Japanese car manufacturer.

The office manager has been responsible for the introduction of new technology into the office and for the introduction of new office procedures. He had hoped that the purchase of a word processor would enable the office staff to use standard replies to customers and suppliers, thus speeding up the office work. However, he has increasingly found the three typists who should make use of the word processor typing individual replies, and all three seem to be very reluctant actually to use the new machinery. He is frustrated by their attitude and is concerned about the cost implications of buying such an expensive item of office machinery and then failing to make use of it.

Activity 7	*a* Draw up a list of the personnel problems which T.K. Engineering faces.
	b Taking each problem in turn, suggest why the problem might have arisen and a policy or policies which the company could pursue in order to alleviate the problem.

The above case study suggests a number of problem areas which a personnel department would be concerned to identify and deal with through specific policies.

Below is a table giving some of the problems which you should have identified and suggestions for possible policies to alleviate the problem. Check these against your own ideas.

Problem	**Suggested policies**
1 New working methods have led to declining job satisfaction.	*Job enlargement*, where one or more tasks at the same level of difficulty as the operator's job are performed.

Job rotation, where operators are moved between various routine tasks.

Job enrichment, where the repetitiveness of the work is reduced and some of the activities of related jobs are incorporated into the enriched jobs. In addition, some responsibility for scheduling and planning their own work may be delegated to operatives.

2 Absenteeism

A *good attendance bonus* could be offered to any worker who does not miss a day's work during a particular week. In addition, policies designed to improve job satisfaction may in themselves reduce absenteeism.

3 Operatives arriving late

Some sort of cash bonus could be offered to those who are not late, or a weekly draw for a prize established where entry is restricted to those at work on time.

Provision of company transport or sponsorship of a car-sharing scheme.

4 High labour turnover

Policies designed to improve job satisfaction may encourage people to stay with the firm.

A long service bonus.

For every five years' service employees could be allocated shares in the company.

Increased holiday entitlements could be offered to those with long-service.

5 Resistance to change (office staff are unwilling to make use of the word processor).

Involve employees who will be affected by technological change in the decision-making and planning surrounding the change.

Ensure that sufficient training is offered prior to the new techology coming into use. Offer some financial incentive.

Personnel policies

The policies which are suggested above are designed to deal with specifically identified problems. There are no universal policies which apply to all organizations. The personnel policies pursued by a particular organization will largely depend upon the objectives of the organization.

The areas in which organizations may define personnel policies include:

1 *Employment policies* eg how many people are required, what quality of staff is needed.
2 *Pay policies* eg determination of levels of pay and differences between jobs.
3 *Training policies* eg to cover the scope of training and the development of specific training schemes; also who should be covered by formal training.
4 *Promotion policies* eg should people within the organization be promoted when vacancies arise, or are there to be specific times when external candidates should be encouraged in order to inject 'new blood' into the organization?
5 *Employee/industrial relations policies* eg determination of the extent to which trade unions are recognized by management and granted negotiation rights on terms and conditions of employment.
6 *Health and safety policies* eg stating clearly the ways in which the organization intends to provide healthy and safe places and systems of work.

Personnel policies, then, are a set of proposals and actions which provide guidelines for dealing with employees.

In most private sector organizations employment policies will be geared to the goals of profit and growth. The planning of the human resources therefore becomes a search for those who will contribute most to the success of the organization. The financial implications of personnel policies have always to be given consideration. Employers have to balance their desire for a contented and stable workforce against the danger of committing themselves to payments and benefits which they may not be able to afford, especially at a later date.

DERBYSHIRE
County Council
Supports Nuclear Free Zones

EQUAL OPPORTUNITIES IN EMPLOYMENT IN DERBYSHIRE COUNTY COUNCIL

This document is prepared to enable the County Council to elaborate simply, but effectively their policies on equal opportunity in employment.

The Policy

The declared policy of the County Council is that with immediate effect, the Council shall operate an equal opportunity of employment policy to ensure that all people who are interested in, or who are working for the County Council, will receive equal treatment in employment regardless of their sex, marital status, sexual orientation, race, creed, colour, or ethnic or national origin or disability.

All employees and potential employees will be made aware of this policy as a matter of course.

Intent

The County Council's philosophy in structure is already based on a non-discriminating policy. However, it is imperative that a systematic and objective appraisal of its practices is now made to ensure that consistency of policy and procedures is rigorously applied, with the definitive objective of equal opportunity. It is clear that in order to achieve equal opportunity, positive action must be taken.

Operation

The Authority has established an Equal Opportunity Working Group where the views of employees, their representatives and other interested parties can contribute towards recommendations to root out any discriminatory practices, wherever they may exist. This Group will recommend notes for guidance to be observed and practised by all employees of the County Council.

Implementation and Progress

Policy will be implemented by a system of progress and monitoring. Each Chief Officer will be responsible for ensuring that all aspects of the policy and practice are being observed.

The collective trade unions whole-heartedly support this policy and representatives of recognised unions have contributed and approved this policy statement.

Statute requires that an employer does not discriminate in the following areas:

    (1)   Sex
    (2)   Colour, race, ethnic or national origins

Nonetheless, without adequate education and training, discrimination is likely to occur notwithstanding the requirements of the law. It is the intent of the County Council to ensure that sufficient education and training is afforded to its members and employees to ensure that discrimination is avoided and the provisions of the law complied with.

Derbyshire County Council's Equal Opportunities statement.

In contrast to organizations led by the goals of profit and growth, some local authorities are developing equal opportunities policies in an attempt to achieve a situation where the manpower within the authority reflects the make-up of the community which it serves. Such an objective will necessarily have implications for manpower planning. Positive action can be taken to train and employ women or members of ethnic minority groups where it can be shown that they are under-represented in particular jobs. As a result, programmes to provide development opportunities have been started, and often such a policy also entails the setting of targets for numbers of women or members of ethnic minorities to be present in particular posts within a certain time. Opposite, for example, is Derbyshire County Council's equal opportunities policy statement.

Manpower needs: demand and supply of labour

The process of planning present and future staff needs is called **manpower planning.** This involves forecasting how much and what types of labour the organization will require, ie the demand for labour. This is done by estimating what the demand for an organization's product or service is going to be and how much the firm will produce or supply.

The demand for labour is said to be a **derived demand**, ie the amount of labour required depends upon or is derived from demand for the product. For example if wearing hats becomes unfashionable then the demand for hats will fall. This will cause the firm to reduce its production level and its demand for machinists who make the hats will also fall. The demand for machinists is therefore dependent upon or derived from the demand for hats.

Manpower planning also involves consideration of the amount of labour which is available, ie the supply of labour, and also how many people are available with the right skills. In addition manpower planners need to be concerned with labour turnover within the organization, ie the rate at which people join the organization and leave it, and with the level of absenteeism.

Using the case study of T.K. Engineering:
a List three factors which would affect the number of
    employees which the firm would need, ie factors
    which influence the firm's demand for labour.
b List three factors which would affect the supply of
    labour available to the firm.

The influences on the demand for and the supply of labour
to T.K. Engineering include some of the following. Check
your own suggestions with the ones below. The factors listed
below could be applied generally to the demand and supply
of labour for most organizations.

Factors influencing the demand for labour

1 *The market demand* Remembering that the demand for
   labour is a derived demand, if the number of car purchases
   increases, then car manufacturers may need to increase
   production. This would increase their demand for
   components, and firms like T.K. Engineering would need
   to expand output: this may require more labour.
   Conversely, if the demand for cars falls, then the demand
   for components would also fall, as would the demand for
   labour.

2 *The technology used by the company* For example, if a firm
   introduces new technology into its production process,
   then this may reduce the manpower required; it may also
   mean that workers with different skills are needed.

3 *The stock levels held by the company* If a firm holds high
   stocks of finished goods, then its labour requirements will
   be greater than if it holds very low stocks. Higher stock
   levels will need more production in order to maintain
   them.

Factors influencing the supply of labour

1 *The national and local levels of employment* Periods of high
   employment can lead to labour shortages, whereas a
   situation of widespread unemployment should mean that
   the supply of labour is high. Of course, although there
   may be many people looking for jobs, if specialist skills are
   required then even in periods of high unemployment
   people with these skills may not be immediately available.

2 *The amount of competition for labour in the area* This will be related not only to the numbers of other employers in the area, but to the type of work they have to offer, pay levels and the general terms and conditions of work.

3 *Union agreements on training etc.* Agreements between trade unions and management on the length of training required for particular jobs may affect the number of people who can actually do that particular job. For example, if a lengthy period of training is required, then this will tend to reduce the supply of labour to that particular occupation.

Wage levels

Salaries and wages are the price which organizations have to pay people in order to obtain work from them. Most organizations will require employees with many different skills and abilities. This means that they will demand labour from a variety of labour markets. For example many jobs do not require any training or previous experience and are therefore largely unskilled, eg manual labour or assembly work. In addition to unskilled labour, an organization may also require skilled workers, such as electricians and people with administrative or management skills who may well have professional qualifications. These different labour markets will give rise to different levels of pay for different jobs.

Demand and supply of labour

We have already examined the major factors which will affect the demand for the supply of labour to particular occupations. It is variations in these factors which produce different rates of pay for different jobs.

The traditional model of labour markets is one where workers are prepared to supply themselves to the labour market if the price (wage) they are paid exceeds their opportunity cost (ie the wage they could have earned in the next best occupation). Employers, on the other hand, are assumed to demand extra workers if the price they have to pay is less than the value of increased output which the worker will create by being employed.

Differences in pay

The pattern of differentials within particular occupational groups and the relativities between occupational groups broadly reflect the demand and supply conditions. The financial controller of a large firm earns more than a shop-floor worker because the job requires specialist skill and years of training. These financial skills are in short supply relative to demand, and therefore organizations are willing to pay more highly in order to attract someone with those skills.

Teachers appear to have slipped down the pay league over the years because the fall in numbers of school-age children has meant a decline in demand relative to the supply of teachers available.

This picture of pay being determined by the market forces of supply and demand shows that the role of differences in pay is to induce labour to move from one type of employment to another. For example a firm whose products are selling well may find itself short of local labour and may therefore offer higher wages to attract employees away from other firms in the area. A shortage of computer programmers may lead to higher earnings being offered to people with computing skills and the good career prospects may then result in greater numbers undertaking training in computing.

| *Activity 9* | Choose a sample of eight to ten jobs. Try to ensure that you choose a mix of occupations in manufacturing and service industries and include unskilled, skilled and professional jobs. Find out the wages received by each of these workers. |

Using the indicators given below, explain the differences in pay levels.

Indicators
Educational qualifications
Length of training
Skills required
Importance of a union or professional association
Working conditions

Payment systems

Individual organizations will have aims and objectives which people are employed to achieve. The basis therefore of a payment system used by an organization should be that it encourages the achievement of the organization's aims and objectives. According to its policy objectives, management is likely to be concerned with the following issues in the establishment of pay levels:

1 the need to attract sufficient suitable employees,
2 obtaining the best performance from employees,
3 encouraging employees to perform more effectively,
4 the need to keep costs at a minimum,
5 the desire to retain effective employees within the organization,
6 ensuring that employees feel fairly rewarded for the jobs they do.

Evaluating employees' performance

One of the major objectives of organizations in relation to their employees is to ensure that they are working effectively for the organization. Staff appraisal involves the measurement of human performance and is concerned with the process of valuing the employee's worth to the organization.

A system of staff appraisal will provide a great deal of information about employees which will help management to take decisions regarding promotions, salary changes, staff transfers, etc. It offers a range of potential benefits to employing organizations including:
1 the provision of detailed information in order to determine pay levels,
2 the improvement of the individual's efficiency,
3 the identification of employees whose abilities are being under-utilized,
4 the identification of weaknesses in individuals, suggesting the need for more training,
5 the identification of skill needs and possible skill shortages.

Methods of performance appraisal

The most commonly used method of performance appraisal uses a results-orientated approach and involves rating an individual's performance against a scale of achievement.

Performance is assessed against specific factors which are considered essential to the efficient performance of the job. The individual's performance is then rated against each of these factors using a scale of achievement, eg a five-point scale might be used:

1 excellent
2 very good
3 good
4 adequate
5 below the required standard.

The sorts of factors which are included in a performance appraisal will of course depend upon the exact nature of the job, but examples of factors often included are:

1 How well does the employee know all aspects of the job?
2 Is the employee prepared to take initiative or do they always need to be told what to do?
3 How accurate is the employee's work?
4 How capable is the employee of communicating with supervisors, colleagues, subordinates, etc?

Appraisal is most commonly carried out by the immediate supervisor of the individual employee concerned. However, many appraisal systems now are more open than they used to be: employees may be shown either all or part of their appraisal reports, or in some cases the employee may actually take the lead and make use of a self-appraisal scheme.

The procedure for conducting performance appraisal involves three main stages:

1 *The report stage* The appraiser draws up a detailed report of the performance of the employee. At this stage the appraisee may also draw up a report.

2 *The communication stage* This usually takes the form of an interview between the individual employee and the person carrying out the appraisal. In broad terms they should discuss the performance of the appraisee and ways in which that performance may be improved for the benefit both of the organization and the individual.

3 *The follow-up stage* This is the stage at which actions resulting from the performance appraisal should take place. Such actions may involve salary review, training proposals, promotion, etc. In order for an appraisal system to have credibility, it is important that there is effective follow-up.

Manpower planning

The manpower planning process attempts to analyse the factors affecting the supply of and the demand for manpower with a view to maximizing the organization's future performance. It is concerned with determining what should or will happen in the future to the organization's requirement for human resources, ie employees. It is only through the process of planning that future potential problems can be identified. For instance, it is useful for an organization to anticipate how many craftsmen it will need in future, particularly as it may take four to five years to train them. If the organization failed to take any action until it needed the craftsmen, and if there were none unemployed in the labour market, then it would have to recruit apprentices and wait four to five years before they were fully productive.

The flow chart below identifies, in general terms, the various stages of the manpower planning process.

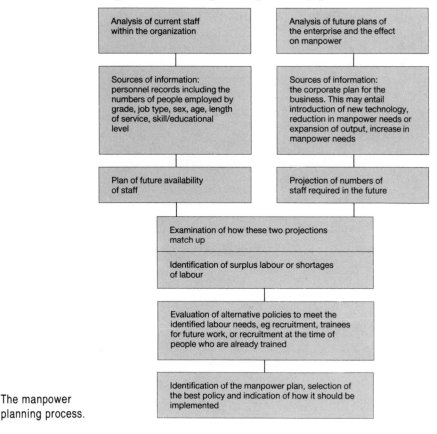

The manpower planning process.

The aims of manpower planning are:
1 to obtain and retain the quantity and quality of manpower required by the organization,
2 to make the best use of the manpower resources available,
3 to anticipate problems arising from having too little labour or too much labour available.

Conclusion

The work in this block has taken you from the consideration of an individual joining an organization to an examination of the sorts of personnel policies which might be pursued, particularly in relation to the acquisition of labour. You will come across other aspects of personnel responsibilities in some of the other blocks of work in this book, including industrial and employee relations.

Summary of skills

The intention of the study involved in this unit is not only to learn facts about organizations, but also to develop skills which will be of use in the business world. This section at the end of each block of work is to indicate the skills areas you should have developed during each activity.

Skills

Skill	Activities in which skill is developed
a Information gathering	1, 3, 4, 6, 7
b Learning and studying	1, 2, 3, 4, 5, 6, 7
c Communicating	1, 3, 4, 5, 6
d Identifying and tackling problems	2, 4, 5, 6
e Design and visual discrimination	4, 5

Links with other units

You should also appreciate the links which exist between your studies in this area and your studies of *People in Organizations* and *Finance*. These activities are related to departmental functions, and information acquisition and presentation, and an appreciation of labour costs and methods of payment.

Block 2
Organizations and the Private Sector

Introduction

In this block you will examine some national figures for the industries and sectors in which people work. Having identified the existence of a public and private sector within the UK economy you will then examine in greater detail the various business organizations which exist in the private sector.

Employment patterns

The table below shows you the industries in which people work in the United Kingdom. Each year the Department of Employment produces these national statistics showing how employment is classified.

Thousands

	1971	1976	1979	1981	1982[2]	1983[2] Males	1983[2] Females	1983[2] All
Agriculture, forestry, and fishing	432	393	368	352	354	261	87	349
Energy and water supply industries[3]	797	721	722	709	686	576	86	662
Extraction of minerals and ores other than fuels, manufacture of metal, mineral products, and chemicals	1,278	1,157	1,128	934	884	659	162	821
Metal goods, engineering, and vehicle industries	3,706	3,329	3,380	2,920	2,772	2,104	546	2,651
Other manufacturing industries	3,102	2,794	2,751	2,368	2,256	1,269	901	2,170
Construction	1,207	1,252	1,253	1,138	1,059	897	120	1,016
Distribution, hotels, catering, and repairs	3,678	3,964	4,252	4,167	4,176	1,942	2,268	4,209
Transport and communication	1,550	1,456	1,473	1,423	1,373	1,067	264	1,332
Banking, finance, insurance business services, and leasing	1,335	1,494	1,663	1,739	1,783	947	890	1,837
Other services	5,035	5,975	6,167	6,122	6,130	2,261	3,903	6,164
All industries and services	22,122	22,543[4]	23,158	21,870	21,473	11,983	9,227	21,210

[1] As at June each year.
[2] Estimates of employees in employment for 1982 and 1983 include an allowance for underestimation.
[3] Includes coal mining.
[4] Includes 8,700 employees who were not allocated to individual industry groups.

Employees in employment by industry. (Source: Social Trends 1985)

a Make a list of all the jobs which people in your group chose to examine in Activity 1 on page 5 in the previous block. If this is not possible, select a range of jobs as indicated in the activity.

b Find out from the individuals concerned the organizations to which the job descriptions relate.

c Taking the list of organizations which you have compiled from your group, classify them into the industrial sectors listed in the table above. If you need a bigger sample you could also include in your list the jobs of part-time students in your group.

d Work out what percentage of your group or sample works in each of the major industrial classifications, eg energy and water supply industries, transport and communication, etc.

What does this tell you about your group or sample?

If you look at the types of jobs done by people in your group or sample, then you will probably find that a large proportion of the group work in the **service sector**, eg banking, insurance, hotel and catering. Your actual findings however will vary depending upon the region in which you are located and the major employers in your area.

a Look again at the table on page 29. Using the 1983 figures for *all employees*, calculate the percentage of employees nationally who work in each of the major industrial areas. Present this information in the form of a bar chart.

b Write a paragraph summarizing your findings and explaining how employees are distributed between the various industries.

c Compare these national findings with the findings for your group or sample.

Your analysis of the national picture of employees in employment should have shown that approximately 30% of employees in employment fall into the category *Other services* (eg public administration, education, medical and health services, etc). The next largest employment category is *Distribution, hotels, catering and repairs* with about 20% of employees. *Banking, finance, insurance, etc,* accounts for 8.7% of employees. We can therefore see that approximately 60%

of all employees work in these three industrial areas. *Metal goods, engineering and vehicle industries*, combined with *Other manufacturing*, between them employ 22.7% of employees. *Construction* accounts for 4.8% of employees and *Transport and Communication* 6.3%. The three sectors of *Agriculture, forestry and fishing, Energy and water supply industries* and *Extraction of minerals and ores, etc*, together employ 8.6% of employees in employment. The pie chart below gives full details of the breakdown.

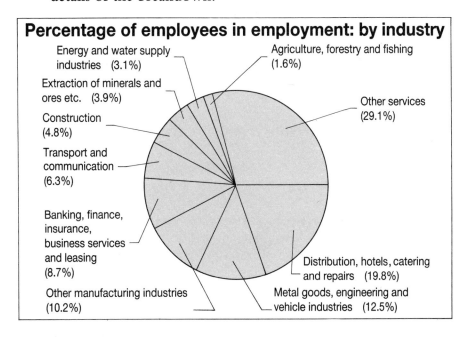

Percentage of employees in employment: by industry

Energy and water supply industries (3.1%)

Agriculture, forestry and fishing (1.6%)

Extraction of minerals and ores etc. (3.9%)

Other services (29.1%)

Construction (4.8%)

Transport and communication (6.3%)

Banking, finance, insurance, business services and leasing (8.7%)

Distribution, hotels, catering and repairs (19.8%)

Other manufacturing industries (10.2%)

Metal goods, engineering and vehicle industries (12.5%)

Activity 3

Look again at the table on page 29.

a How have the numbers of people working in the different industrial sectors changed over the last twelve years?

b What has happened to the total number of employees in employment?

The total number of employees in employment in the United Kingdom increased by just over one million between 1971 and 1979, before falling over the next four years. Between June 1971 and June 1983 the number employed in manufacturing industries fell by nearly 2.5 million. In 1971 *Metal goods, engineering and vehicle industries* and *Other manufacturing industries* combined, employed 31% of the total employees in employment, but by 1983 they provided jobs

for only 23% of employees. Between 1979 and 1983 the
number of employees in the *Metal goods, engineering and
vehicle industries* fell by 22% and the number in *Construction*
by 19%. In the service industries, which expanded by almost
two million between 1971 and 1979, the number of
employees fell slightly between 1979 and 1983, although in
banking, finance, insurance, etc, the numbers increased by
10% over this latter period.

Changes in employment levels and patterns

The employment figures given above reflect the decline in
manufacturing industry's share of employment. This shift to
the service sector in employment has been taking place for a
number of decades. Already no more than one in four
workers is engaged in manufacturing and this falling share of
total employment is likely to continue.

A problem arises when jobs do not emerge in service
occupations at anything like the rate of their disappearance
from manufacturing. The service sector itself cannot remain
immune from the applications of new technology. Today's
microelectronic and information-oriented technology is
applicable to many service sector activities, eg
microcomputer applications in insurance and banking.

If the growth in jobs in new areas of industry is slower than
the rate at which jobs are being lost in other areas, then
unemployment results. The level of unemployment
nationally in the UK has been rising steadily. In 1984 the
national ratio of registered unemployed to registered job
vacancies was 25 : 1 (ie for every one job vacancy there were
twenty-five people registered as unemployed). Because
different regions of the country rely on different industries
there are great differences in the level of unemployment
between areas. In the West Midlands in 1984 there was one
vacancy for every thirty-five jobless, in Northern Ireland,
one vacancy for every one hundred and fifty jobless, while in
the south-east there was one vacancy for every fifteen jobless.

So far in this block we have concentrated on examining
where people work through the industrial classification used
by the Department of Employment. Organizations and areas
of work can however be classified in many different ways.

The public and private sectors

Most business organizations can be divided into two broad categories, depending on their form of ownership. So within the UK economy we have both a public sector and a private sector.

Organizations in the public sector are public in the sense that they are controlled by central or local government, financed by public funds and managed by people selected by government. Broadly, public sector organizations can be grouped under three main headings: public corporations (including nationalized industries, eg the National Coal Board), government departments, eg the Department of Health and Social Security, and local authorities, eg Bedfordshire County Council. For a more detailed examination of this sector of the economy refer to Block 3.

The private sector includes all those organizations owned by individuals or groups of shareholders with the main purpose of making a profit and thereby obtaining a return on their investment. A variety of organizations of different size and with different structures is found within the private sector. Some are very large and wealthy, eg Imperial Chemical Industries (ICI), while others are very small, eg the local newsagent.

Activity 4	Taking the list of jobs which you obtained from your group for Activity 1, draw up two lists, one including those in the private sector and the other those in the public sector.

If you have any difficulty categorizing the jobs, read on further in this section and the distinction between public and private sector organizations should become clearer.

Activity 5	The chart on page 36 shows you the number of people in employment by sector and clearly indicates those employed in the private sector and those in the public sector.

a How many people work in the public sector and how many in the private sector?

b Which provides the greater source of employment?

c How has the share of employment between the two sectors changed over the twenty-two year period?

Northern Foods

REPORT AND ACCOUNTS
1985

Northern Foods plc

Chairman's Statement

I am somewhat disappointed to announce a small increase in pre-tax profits which have moved to £55.4 million from £53.3 million in the previous comparable twelve month period. In the first half we reported a small reduction in profits but in the second six months we showed a twelve per cent increase. This was achieved in perhaps the most difficult trading conditions we have faced for a decade. Earnings per share have increased from 18.72p to 19.26p per share.

The directors are recommending a final dividend of 3.0p per share making a total for the year of 7.25p per share compared to 6.75p per share for the comparable period in 1984.

A more detailed review of operations is given on page 4 but it is appropriate to comment on one or two highlights of the year.

In the United Kingdom profits have fallen mainly due to difficulties in the meat and milk divisions. By contrast the milling and baking division achieved a substantial improvement in profits.

The Government's policy for decontrol of the milk industry came into effect from 1st January 1985, with the withdrawal of the involvement of the Ministry of Agriculture. The trade now negotiates prices directly with the Milk Marketing Board, which continues its role as sole supplier.

In the United States of America our progress was mainly a result of currency gains. We have virtually completed the re-organisation of Bluebird (renamed Prestige Foods Corporation) through the disposal of Patrick Cudahy and the withdrawal from all hog slaughtering. The re-organisation provisions made in 1984 have been adequate.

Capital Expenditure
New investment in the year to 31st March 1985 amounted to £45 million. Expenditure in the new financial year will be similar.

Recent Events
In recent weeks there have been major developments in the two leading United Kingdom activities the benefit of which will not emerge fully until the year to 31st March 1987.

At the end of March we purchased the liquid milk business of Express Dairies in the north of England for a consideration of approximately £51 million. This will substantially increase our share of the liquid milk market and will lead to further rationalisation.

More recently we have acquired Bowyers (Wiltshire) Limited from Unigate for a consideration of approximately £21 million. Bowyers is a leading brand for sausage and pies. This acquisition establishes our meat group as a major force in the United Kingdom food manufacturing industry with annual sales of £300 million and some 8,000 employees.

In the United States of America we have acquired the Sears, Roebuck and Company franchise to provide consumer cleaning services throughout the western United States. The acquisition establishes Keystone Foods Corporation as the national Sears concessionaire for consumer cleaning services.

Since the year end we have reached agreement with Mansfield Brewery whereby it will acquire North Country Breweries for a consideration of £42 million. It is regrettable that this decision involves the cessation of brewing in Hull but it had become increasingly difficult for our company to compete effectively with national brands.

Current Trading
These developments, combined with improved trading in the United Kingdom and further progress in the United States of America, will provide sound growth in profits for the year to 31st March 1986. The first few weeks of trading in the new financial year are better than budget and comfortably ahead of the previous year.

Management
In December 1984 Michael Morgan, who has been with the group since May 1967, was appointed to the board as personnel director. We have also announced that Chris Ball, former Chairman of Unigate Dairy Holdings, is to join the board from September 1st as managing director – UK. At the same time Christopher Haskins becomes group managing director.

It is with sadness we report the death last year of Gilbert Wright who for some years was vice chairman of the group.

Employees
I would like to thank all our employees on both sides of the Atlantic for the tremendous efforts they have made in the business during this very difficult year of trading.

Shareholders will see that a further profit sharing allocation of £1.5 million has been made in respect of the year to 31st March 1985. An increasing number of United Kingdom employees qualify for inclusion in this scheme.

The Future
With the recent developments and good current trading your board is facing the future with confidence.

Nicholas Horsley

Nicholas Horsley *chairman*

18th June 1985

Reports from public limited companies: a Northern Foods report and accounts (extract).

3

THE BOOTS COMPANY PLC

THE BOOTS COMPANY PLC
Report and Accounts 1985

THE BOOTS COMPANY PLC

Statement by the chairman

I should liké to begin my first statement by paying tribute to my predecessor, Dr Peter Main, who retired on 31st March 1985 after twenty-eight years' distinguished service with the Company. Under his chairmanship, the group made substantial progress. We are greatly indebted to him and we wish him every happiness in the future.

Group sales for the year were £2,033·1m, an increase of 10·9%, and profits before tax increased by 15·3% to £190·3m. Excluding the surplus on disposal of properties (£8·9m), profits were up by 22·1%.

The Industrial Division had a sales increase of 13·7% but profits grew by only 3%. Pharmaceuticals had a good year, the gains coming from our overseas companies, but the future is uncertain because of government policies in many countries. In the UK further, even more damaging, measures have been imposed. The introduction of the limited list to National Health Service prescribing has been well publicised, and the further severe reduction in the allowed return on capital to a level which is quite insufficient for a high risk, research-based industry, must be expected to have a serious impact on the level of investment by pharmaceutical companies in this country.

We were delighted that our Research Department received The Queen's Award for Technological Achievement for the discovery and development of ibuprofen, our world-renowned antirheumatic. This is welcome recognition for an outstanding product and all who have worked for its success over the years.

Our Consumer Products business had a disappointing year largely as a result of severe problems in certain overseas markets, particularly Kenya and Nigeria. However, the successful launch of over-the-counter ibuprofen through our licensee in the United States, and our increased sales of Nurofen in the United Kingdom, give us confidence for an improved result in the current year.

In September, a number of important changes to the composition of your Board took place. Mr I M G Prosser was appointed to the Board as a Non-Executive Director. Mr Prosser is Vice Chairman and Group Managing Director of Bass PLC.

Mr G M Hourston became Deputy Managing Director of Boots The Chemists, and Mr A H Hawksworth was appointed to the Board to replace him as Staff Director. Mr B H C Theobald took over the new post of Group Corporate Development Director. Mr M F Ruddell was appointed to the Board and brings with him considerable retail merchandise and marketing expertise. I believe that these changes have strengthened your Board considerably.

The year under review has been one of considerable change within the Company and much has been achieved. Capital expenditure rose sharply to £93m (£59·9m last year), covering enhancements to our retail business and our production and research facilities at home and abroad. Investment will continue to increase over the next two years.

Robert Gunn

ROBERT GUNN
CHAIRMAN

A Boots report and accounts (extract).

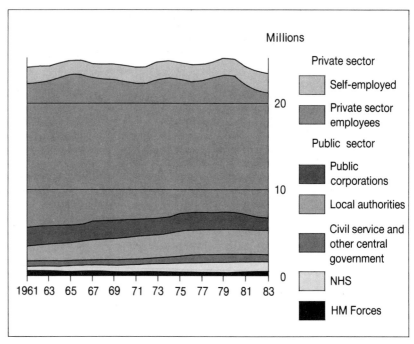

Millions

Private sector

Self-employed

Private sector employees

Public sector

Public corporations

Local authorities

Civil service and other central government

NHS

HM Forces

20

10

0

1961 63 65 67 69 71 73 75 77 79 81 83

People in employment, by sector. (Source: Social Trends 1985)

Of the total number of people in employment in 1983 (23.7 million), 71% (16.8 million) were in the private sector. The remaining 6.9 million were employed in the public sector, employment in the sector being split between 1.7 million (7%) employed in public corporations and 5.2 million (22%) in central and local government.

Although the private sector clearly provides the greatest source of employment, the importance of the public sector, existing alongside the private sector, means that the UK economy is known as a **mixed economy**. In other words, some of our economic resources are publicly owned and some are privately owned.

Public or private ownership?

In recent years government in the UK has aimed at bringing about a new 'mix' in the economy. They are placing much greater reliance on the private sector and the operation of market forces according to which prices are a gauge of how much consumers are prepared to buy and how much producers are willing to sell of various goods and services.

One of the main ways in which government has attempted to reduce the size of the public sector is through a policy of **privatization**, as explained below.

Activity 6	Make a list of any services which used to be provided by organizations within the public sector but which are now provided by private sector organizations.

Public sector activities can be returned to the private sector by a number of means. For example shares in British Telecom (BT) were sold to private individuals, so that BT is now a public limited company (PLC) and no longer a nationalized industry. Services like the cleaning of schools and other public buildings, and the collection of refuse, previously carried out by local authority employees, have been contracted out to private companies in some areas. British Rail hotel properties have been sold off to private owners. All these activities alter the degree of the mix between the private and public sector.

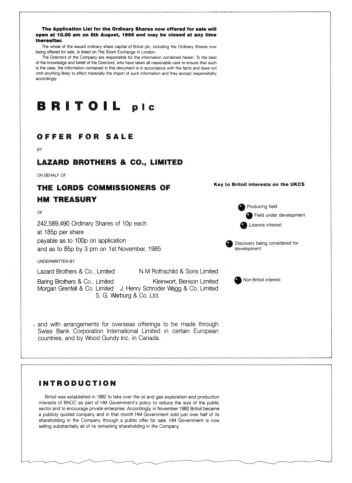

A Britoil offer for sale of shares.

The main arguments put forward in favour of the move towards private ownership are that the private sector provides greater competition and therefore organizations operate more efficiently.

Activity 7 Working in groups look back again at the table on page 29. For each industry listed, try to think of a specific organization which operates in each of the industries. Make use of your knowledge of local industry as well as national industry. Make a note of the names. Which belong to the public sector and which to the private sector?

As we have seen, some parts of industry are publicly owned and others privately owned. A variety of organizations with different structures and of different sizes is found within the private sector. The size of the business and the type of work it carries out determines the type of business organization. The main types are given below.

Private sector organizations

Type of organization	Nature of business
Sole trader	Small local shop, eg butcher, newsagent; a plumber or electrician in business on his own
Partnership	The professions, eg architects, solicitors, accountants
Private limited company	Small firms, eg a local building firm; larger firms may also be private limited companies
Public limited company (PLC)	Large firms, eg Marks and Spencer PLC, National Westminster Bank PLC, Imperial Group PLC
Co-operatives	Retail co-operatives, eg the Co-op; producer co-operatives, eg Meriden

Activity 8	Identify a small local business which is owned by the person who runs it, eg a local shop. Try to find out the following details:

  a Where does the owner obtain finance from to run the business?
  b What would happen if the business were unprofitable? Who would be responsible for any debts?
  c Who decides how the business is run, eg what is sold, which suppliers are used, etc?

It is likely that the organization which you identified for Activity 8 was either a sole trader or partnership. In order to make clear the distinction between the two we will now examine their main characteristics.

Sole traders

Sole traders are businesses owned by private individuals who have to provide all the finance (perhaps through loans), take all decisions relating to running the business, and assume all the risks.

A sole trader is in full control of the business, setting objectives, determining policy and taking the day-to-day decisions. It is often this independence which attracts individuals to set up in business on their own. If the business goes well, all the profits go to the owner; if it goes badly then any losses would also have to be borne by the owner. This may even entail the sale of personal assets in order to pay off the debts of the business; this is known as having unlimited liability. Because the individual has sole responsibility for the business, there is no legal obligation to make the accounts publicly available.

Ownership and control in such businesses is vested in one person who enjoys all the fruits of success and therefore has a substantial incentive to run the firm efficiently.

The major problem faced by sole traders is the strict limitation on their ability to acquire finance or capital for expansion. Finance is restricted to the individual's own resources and whatever sums can be borrowed. The major external sources of finance available include those listed on the following pages.

Overdraft facilities

This is where the individual is given a specific level of credit which they can draw on when they wish. The bank will make the money available through the customer's current account. If part of the overdraft facility is not used, ie they do not borrow all the money the bank is willing to lend, then interest will only be paid on the amount borrowed. Overdrafts provide a way of borrowing short-term and are usually provided to facilitate working capital to pay day-to-day bills which cannot be met because customers have not yet paid up.

Bank loans

If a longer-term loan is required, then banks will lend a given amount with interest charged on the entire sum from the day it is borrowed. Repayments are either in instalments over a period, or in total after a set time. The loan may be **secured** or **unsecured**. If it is secured then the bank will hold security or something of value, eg deeds to property which it can then turn into cash if the borrower fails to repay the loan. In making loans to small businesses, banks will require extensive information about the background of the business, the nature of the venture, the market, and expected sales and profitabiliy, together with projected cash flows, both short and long term. An example of the sorts of information required by banks is given below.

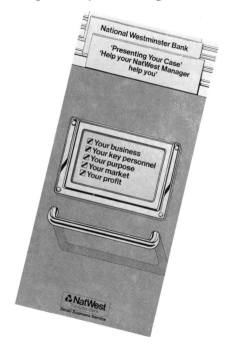

Presenting your case to your Bank Manager

Presenting a good case to your bank manager is the best possible first step to obtaining the finance your business needs. Nothing impresses the banker more than a well thought-out case with all the relevant facts properly marshalled, and clearly presented.

This leaflet is specifically laid out in check-list form for quick and easy reference, to reduce time and concern over approach and presentation. If you're not thinking of borrowing at the moment, keep a copy handy, ready for the next business opportunity you spot.

There are over 3,200 branches of NatWest capable of helping the small businessman understand the 'rules of the game'. If you have any doubts about your presentation, or need some help preparing, say, the cash flow, or if you would simply appreciate a second opinion prior to your formal request, call in and ask, it can only help. A poor presentation of a sound proposition can seriously affect the prospects of obtaining finance by prolonging the discussions and causing frustration all round.

Finally, don't be put off by the size of the check list, it's meant to be comprehensive to help

you as much as possible. There is no 'ideal' plan to cover all the details of every proposition, and many of the points shown may well be irrelevant to your case.

Tips

Imagine you're the salesman and the banker is the customer. Try and put yourself in the shoes of the banker, would you lend money on the basis of your presentation? Bear in mind that the banker is also running a business and trying to make a profit.

Remember optimism is not enough, try and substantiate your figures, you must not expect them to be taken on trust.

Keep an open mind about equity type finance. If the risk to the lender is substantially greater than your own, it may well be the right answer.

Make your presentation as clear and concise as possible, not all the points need be documented, but have your answers prepared.

Make your approach in plenty of time, particularly if long term finance is involved, sending a copy of your documentation to the banker prior to your meeting.

Our booklet 'Start Up and Go with NatWest', which is available from your local branch, is designed to help you make the best possible presentation of your case to the bank manager and the best possible job of getting your business up and running.

For help in preparing a cashflow and profit forecast our booklet 'Know Your Own Business', also available from your local branch, is highly recommended.

Check List

About you

☐ Very brief synopsis for your own banker, detailed for approach to others: age, education, experience.

☐ Personal means eg property, liabilities eg guarantees. Other business connections.

☐ For a type of business new to you, or start-up situation, outline experience, ability and factors leading up to your decision.

Your business

☐ Brief details of: when established, purpose then and now, how the business has evolved, main factors contributing to progress.

☐ Reputation, current structure and organisation. Internal accounting system.

☐ Past 3 years audited accounts if available, and latest position.

☐ Up to date Profit and Loss figures, including details of withdrawals.

☐ Up to date liquid figures, ie debtors, creditors, stock, bank balance etc.

☐ Borrowing history and existing commitments, eg HP, leasing loans. Bankers.

☐ Description of major assets, and any changes.

Your key personnel

☐ Age, qualifications, experience, competence of directorate/senior management. Directors' bankers.

☐ Someone to run the business in your absence. Could they cope in an emergency?

☐ List of principal shareholders/relationships.

Your purpose

☐ Explain fully your business plan, the use to which the money will be put, eg expansion, diversification, start-up.

☐ Describe the practical aspects involved and the how and when of implementation.

☐ Diagrams, sketches, photographs etc are usually helpful, eg property purchase and conversion to your use.

☐ Consider: planning permission, legal restrictions, government policy.

☐ Contingency plans for set backs: reliability of supplies/raw materials/ alternative sources, other factors outside your control, eg weather.

☐ Relevance to existing operations, opportunity for shared overheads, disruption of current business.

☐ Personnel, are more staff required, availability of specialist skills/training. Management ability for expanded/different operation?

Your Market

☐ Estimated demand, short and long term. External verification of market forecasts, eg from trade associations, market research publications.

☐ Competition, who from, likely developments.

☐ Describe your competitive advantages, eg quality, uniqueness, pricing (justify) location – local/national.

☐ Marketing included in costings?

☐ If new, or technology based or highly specialised business – detail and perspective necessary. NB A banker does not need to know how it works (though he may be interested), just that it does, is reliable, and has good sales prospects.

Your profit

☐ Demonstrate how profits will be made, include detailed breakdown of costings, timing, projected sales, orders already held.

☐ Profit projections should attempt to cover the period of a loan, however sketchy.

☐ Everything included in costings? Eg tax, stamp duty, legal fees, bank interest.

The amount

☐ State precisely the amount and type of finance required and when it will be needed. Is type of finance correct? Eg overdraft to finance working capital, term loan for capital expenditure.

☐ Is the amount requested sufficient? Eg increased working capital requirements/ margin for unforeseen circumstances.

☐ Detail the amount and form of your contribution to the total cost.

☐ Justify all figures – cash flow forecast for next 12 months: show maximum range. All out-goings considered eg net VAT, holiday pay, bank interest and repayments, personal drawings.

Repayment

☐ Relate projected profitability and cash flow to expected repayments. Justify fully the term requested. Is it long enough?

☐ How quickly will the business generate cash? Is a repayment 'holiday' necessary and what turnover needs to be achieved to break-even?

☐ Consider the worst situation, feasibility of contingency plans, irretrievable losses.

☐ Interest rate – effect of variation in base rate.

Security

☐ What assets are/will be available as security?

☐ Are any assets already used for security elsewhere?

continued

☐ Independent/realistic valuation of assets offered. Leasehold considerations, any unusual features/saleability. Support for guarantees.

☐ Agreement of other interested parties/realistic awareness of loss of asset.

☐ Insurance – life, property, business.

NatWest Business Services

Current Account Service including

Cheque book

Direct debits/Standing orders

Statements produced regularly or on request

Night safes to keep your takings safe after trading hours

'Autopay': a simple method of sending regular trade and wage payments to a variety of different recipients

Foreign currency, travel cheques for your visits abroad.

Deposit Account

Interest earning account to hold spare cash and to set aside money for future bills such as VAT.

Lending Services

Overdraft

The simplest way of borrowing to cover your fluctuating day to day requirements.

Loans

For your longer term borrowing requirements.

Business Development Loans

Simply arranged loans at a fixed rate of interest which means you know in advance the cost of borrowing.

Small Firms Loan Guarantee Scheme

A joint scheme whereby the Department of Industry guarantees a proportion of the loan in approved cases.

NatWest/Council for Small Industries in Rural Areas Lending Scheme

A joint scheme offering special terms for small businesses in rural areas of England.

NatWest/European Coal & Steel Community Lending Scheme

A loan scheme offering preferential fixed interest rates, linked to job creation, for small businesses in coal and steel closure areas.

NatWest/European Investment Bank Lending Scheme

A loan scheme offering preferential fixed interest rates to eligible small businesses in the manufacturing and tourism industries in assisted areas.

Franchising

Structured financial packages are available for people considering buying into leading franchises.

Other Financial Services

Factoring

A means of obtaining immediate cash upon the issue of your

invoices whilst giving protection against bad debts.
...service available from Credit Factoring International Ltd.

Leasing and Lease Purchase

Alternative ways of acquiring machinery and other assets without reducing working capital.
...services available from Lombard North Central PLC.

Payroll Service

Computerised payment of wages and handling of all the related paperwork including changes in legislation.

Accounting Services

Computerised administration of time consuming bookwork, such as sales and purchase ledgers, including preparation of VAT returns.
...services available from Centre-file Limited.

Insurance Services

Life, pension and business protection policies to give you

and your family peace of mind now and for the future.
...services available from National Westminster Insurance Services Limited.

Trust & Tax Services

Providing expert advice and administration services on all aspects of tax, estate planning and company pension funds.
...services available from National Westminster Trust and Tax Services.

Import/Export Services

Dealing with your payments and receipts in foreign currency or sterling and providing various means of financing each transaction.

Foreign Exchange

If you get paid, or need to make payments, in foreign currencies the Bank will buy or sell the currency to meet your requirements, and you can also protect yourself against future adverse movements in exchange rates using forward contracts or currency accounts.

In addition to these and other NatWest services we offer:

Information on Government Grants, market conditions in different industries and opportunities for overseas trade.

Advice on the general financial requirements of businesses, including the Small Business Digest which is available quarterly, free of charge.

Just contact your local NatWest Manager for further details – **we're here to help you.**

NWB 3386 May 1985
National Westminster Bank PLC, 41 Lothbury, London EC2P 2BP

Designed by David Pocknell's Company

An example of the kinds of loan and financial services available to small businesses. (Reproduced courtesy of the National Westminster Bank PLC.)

Trade credit

This is an important source of finance for the smaller firm and is most often used to buy stocks of raw materials, components, goods, etc. The supplier supplies goods on credit terms, agreeing that payment will be made at a later date, usually within thirty days.

Equipment leasing

Instead of using a medium-term loan to buy new assets, many assets can be acquired through leasing. Under a leasing agreement, the leasing company provides the equipment, eg photocopiers, vehicles, machinery, and then leases them to the customer for an agreed period at an agreed rental. Sometimes the leasing company provides a service and maintenance contract for an extra charge. The asset remains the property of the leasing company. Although this may be quite an expensive method of acquiring assests, it has the advantage of allowing firms to keep up to date with changes in technology, whereas the purchase of assets may mean holding onto out-of-date equipment in order to ensure costs are recovered.

Hire purchase

This method of financing is also used for the purchase of equipment and applies to businesses in much the same way as to the retail trade. A deposit is paid by the purchaser who receives the use of the equipment immediately; regular payments are then made and on completion of these the equipment becomes the purchaser's property. When a firm buys goods on hire purchase it is, in effect, obtaining a loan from the finance company which supplies the funds to support the hire purchase scheme.

Government help

The Enterprise Allowance Scheme offers a payment of £40 per week for up to one year to people who have been unemployed and wish to become self-employed. The payment is designed to help them in the first year of the enterprise and to compensate them for the loss of benefit.

| Activity 9 | Find out what sort of assistance your local authority offers to small enterprises in the area. If there are |

GRANTS AND ASSISTANCE FOR INDUSTRY AND COMMERCE

HOW THE CITY COUNCIL CAN HELP

City of Nottingham

The present policies of Nottingham City Council's Economic Development Sub-Committee combined with the activities of the Industrial and Commercial Development Unit have resulted in various forms of financial assistance; grants; incentive schemes and services being available to the business community.

Such schemes are either funded directly by the City Council as part of its commitment to help create and preserve jobs or in conjunction with the Department of the Environment — taking full advantage of the grants offered by Central Government to help stimulate investment and improvements in the Inner City areas.

The types of assistance and services available include Industrial Improvement Area Grants; Rent Relief Grants; a Business Loans Scheme; the provision of small industrial units as part of an Advance Factory Programme; an Enterprise Workshop scheme to help small business get started and "Operation Clean-Up" grants for building exteriors. Assistance is also given with locating premises, including the availability of property, sites and developments in both the public and commercial sectors.

The purpose of this booklet is to highlight *all* the help which is available to industry and commerce through the City Council and indicate the contact points in the various Departments involved where approaches for further details and information can be made.

An example of local authority assistance to small enterprises.

incentives available, design a leaflet, using one piece of
A4 paper, giving details of the incentives, for circulation
to local businesses.

Many local authorities also offer incentives and assistance to
local firms. Publicity for a typical local authority is shown
on the previous page. A variety of assistance and services are
available to business:

Rent Relief Grants Rent relief grants are aimed at assisting
either new enterprises or existing, recently formed, small
businesses. The grants provide 75% of the rent in the first six
months, falling to 50% of the rent in the second six months,
and 25% in the second year.

Business Loans Scheme This type of scheme is seen as a last
resort but can provide funds for valid proposals which have
failed to attract finance from the usual sources.

Enterprise Workshop Scheme This scheme provides small,
inexpensive rented accommodation coupled with on-the-spot
advice covering all aspects of running a business.

Partnerships

A partnership can have from two to twenty members.
Forming a partnership obviously can increase the availability
of finance as each partner contributes to the capital of the
business. Other sources of finance available to partnerships
include bank loans and overdrafts, trade credit, equipment
leasing, hire purchase, and central and local government
initiatives.

The Partnership Act 1890 lays down the legal rules which
govern the operation of partnerships. Any profits or losses
will normally be shared in an agreed proportion depending
on the individual's contribution to the partnership. The
partners agree on the day-to-day running of the business,
although some members can be 'sleeping' partners in that
they do not actively participate in the business.

The partners have unlimited liability, which means that each
partner is jointly liable with the other partners for the debts
of the business, and like sole traders there is no obligation for
a partnership to publish its accounts.

Co-operatives

You will probably be familiar with retail co-operatives which are members of the Co-operative Wholesale Society (CWS). Features of retail co-ops are:

1 They must be registered as self-governing bodies under the Industrial and Provident Societies' Act 1965.
2 The members are the customers who use the shops.
3 The Society's shares are not quoted on the Stock Exchange. Any number of shares may be issued and members receive fixed interest on these shares. They also receive a dividend on their purchases, usually in the form of trading stamps.
4 Members elect a committee of management who employ officials to manage the day-to-day running of the business.

The other type of co-operative which is becoming more common in the UK is the worker co-operative. In such organizations the workers own the business, make all the decisions, and share the profits. In the 1970's, several large worker co-operatives were set up in attempts to rescue failing private businesses such as the Meriden Co-operative and Kirby Manufacturing and Engineering (KME).

In 1985 there were over 1000 worker co-operatives employing over 9000 workers. The majority have tended to be small service businesses, although there is now evidence that worker co-operatives are moving into new areas including manufacturing and the 'new' technologies. The Co-operative Development Agency is a government funded body with local branches assisting workers in setting up and running co-operatives.

Private Limited Companies and Public Limited Companies

The joint stock company is the most important form of business organization in the U.K. It consists of an association of people who contribute towards a joint stock of capital in order to carry on a business with the objective of making a profit.

There are two types of joint stock company, the private company and the public company. The public companies are very large units and must be recognizable from their title which must have the words 'public limited company' at the end of their name; this is often shortened to PLC, eg National Westminster Bank PLC. The basic distinction between a private and a public company is that a public company can offer shares for sale to the general public, whereas a private company cannot.

We can now go on to examine the characteristics of companies by looking at the development of a partnership carrying out building work.

Partnership to Private Limited Company

Des Handley and Michael Murphy have been operating very successfully as a partnership and have become established and successful builders in their locality. They have the opportunity to undertake larger jobs but cannot do so without more manpower and equipment. Their other problem is that they have insufficient capital: their finance is restricted.

They decide to look at the possibility of becoming a private limited company. This would allow them to introduce new shareholders to take part-ownership of the firm and would directly increase the capital available. Although they would not be able to sell shares to the general public, both partners have members of family and business associates who have expressed an interest in the plan. The shareholders would have limited liability for the debts of the firm, only being liable for debts up to the value of their shareholding.

Naturally all the new shareholders would expect to receive a proportion of the firm's profits in return for their interest in the firm. So the partners would no longer receive all the profits but neither would they be liable for all the losses.

If they decide to go ahead and form a private limited company, then the firm must go through the process of incorporation, complying with the Companies Act 1948.

In order to do this, two documents must be prepared.

1 *The Memorandum of Association*

This document regulates the company's dealings with the outside world and is signed by all those wishing to associate together as a company. It contains the following clauses:

a Title of the company, which must include *limited*.
b Address of its registered office.
c The objectives of the company, ie a statement of the areas of trade in which the company will be engaged. This ensures that the shareholders' money will not be used for other activities.
d The amount of share capital to be issued. This is the amount of finance that can be raised by selling shares to the company's members.
e A statement that the liability of the company is limited.
f A statement by all signing the memorandum that they wish to form a company and will purchase the shares allotted to them.
g The names of the directors and company secretary.

2 *The Articles of Association*

This document governs the company's internal operation and management. It contains details of the rights of shareholders, the powers and duties of the managing director and other directors, and the frequency and type of company meetings.

These two documents must then be sent to the Registrar of Companies. Providing the documents are in order, a **Certificate of Incorporation** will be issued and the firm can trade as a private limited company.

| Activity 10 | During the period leading up to the decision to form a company, the two partners disagree about the future development of the business. Des Handley prefers to remain a partnership whereas Michael Murphy is keen to expand the business. They decide to have a final meeting to thrash out the issue of whether or not to become a company.

Placing yourself in Michael's position prepare some notes of the arguments which you will put to Des. |

Companies and their financing

The initial capital of companies, whether public or private, is raised by the issuing of shares. This has the effect of giving the shareholder a long-term interest in the company. Long-term finance can also be raised by the issuing of a debenture: this is simply a document given by a company to acknowledge its debt to the holder. There are many terms used in connection with the financing of companies which it is useful to be familiar with:

1 *Nominal (Authorized) capital*

This indicates the value of shares that a company is authorized to issue and is stated in the Memorandum of Association of a company.

2 *Issued capital*

This indicates the value of capital in the form of shares which have actually been issued to shareholders.

3 *Paid-up capital*

This is the amount of capital which has actually been paid up on the shares issued. Shares need not be fully paid for when they are issued. For example, a company may issue £1 shares by asking for 20p on application and 40p on allotment (ie when the shares are actually made available to the applicant). It may decide not to call up the remaining 40p per share for some considerable time.

4 *Ordinary shares*

The ordinary share capital of a company is usually referred to as the **equity** of the company. The **dividend** (earnings) on ordinary shares is not fixed and depends upon the profitability of the company and the policy of the directors with regard to the amount of profit to be retained by the company for investment purposes. Therefore, if high profits are made, ordinary shareholders are likely to get a reasonable dividend paid to them. On the other hand, if the company makes a loss, then the ordinary shareholders will receive nothing. The payments to ordinary shareholders are made after all other claims have been met, eg payments to preference shareholders (see (5) below).

Ordinary shares are the riskiest type of investment as dividends may fluctuate from year to year, but in addition the value of the shares themselves will also vary according to the performance of the company. An ordinary shareholder in a well-managed company which is making high profits will receive a good return on the investment and the nominal value of the shares will rise (eg a £1 ordinary share could rise to have a market value of £1.70). However the opposite is also true: a company whose performance is poor may find the value of its ordinary shares falling.

The risk which the ordinary shareholder takes is reflected in the amount of control which they have over the company's business. This control is exercised through the voting rights which ordinary shareholders have, enabling them to attend shareholders meetings and to voice their opinion and vote on major issues involving the company.

5 *Preference shares*

As the name implies, holders of preference shares are given preference in the payment of profits, ie they are paid before ordinary shareholders. The holder of a preference share is entitled to a fixed amount of dividend (usually expressed as a fixed percentage of their nominal value). A holder of a £100, 6% preference share is entitled to a return of £6 per annum. A preference share is therefore a relatively safe investment with a fixed reward, no matter how small or large the company's profit is. If the company makes a loss, then no dividend has to be paid unless the preference shares are classed as **cumulative preference shares**, in which case if the company's profits are not sufficient to declare a dividend, the shortfall must be made up out of the profits of subsequent years.

In general then, even if the company has a very profitable year, the holder of preference shares will receive no more than the fixed rate of return, unless they hold the class of share termed **participating preference share**. This class of share entitles the holder to the fixed return plus an additional share in the profits. Preference shares do not usually carry voting rights since their income is not directly dependent upon the level of profits; however, in a situation where the dividend has not been paid, then voting rights may be granted.

6 Debentures

Trading companies can borrow money by means of issuing a debenture or a series of debentures. Investors who purchase debentures are making a loan to the company and become a creditor of the company (ie someone to whom the business owes money) rather than an owner. The rate of interest on debentures is fixed. The holders of these securities are often given rights which add to the security of the loan. The company may offer certain assets as security so that in the event of default by the company, the debenture holders may seize and sell these assets in order to secure repayment of the loan.

In addition to shares and debentures which are used to raise large sums of money, companies can also make use of the various other sources of finance available to other business organizations, eg loans, overdrafts, leasing, trade credit, etc.

Raising share capital

As has already been indicated, the major distinction between a private limited company and a public limited company is that a private company cannot invite the public to subscribe to a share issue. This restriction effectively limits the capacity of a private company to raise large amounts of capital, as it has to rely on individuals who are aware of its existence and who therefore may be interested in buying shares.

In order for a public company to acquire its initial capital or increase its issued capital, it will issue a prospectus to advertise the company and to induce the public to subscribe for shares of debentures. The prospectus is advertised in national newspapers and contains information on the company's financial position, trading prospects and recent results. The advertisement will invite the public to apply for shares and a closing date for applications is indicated.

Multinational corporations

A multinational company (MNC) is a company that has a legally identifiable base in more than one country and which carries out its operations in a large number of countries. Multinationals actually establish production facilities in these different countries rather than just engage in foreign trade.

1. **INTRODUCTION**

The Company was incorporated on the 1st March 1985 and has been purchased by the Directors to acquire the Old Swan Inn, with the brewery attached, at No. 89 Halesowen Road, Netherton, Nr. Dudley, West Midlands, more affectionately and better known as Ma Pardoe's. The adjacent premises, Nos. 85 and 87, together with the goodwill, assets, and trade names of the existing business are also being acquired. The Company contracted to purchase the business on the 20th March 1985 conditionally upon the issue of a Trading Certificate. Completion is due to take place on the 26th April 1985. The Company intends to develop the existing home brew public house at the Old Swan Inn, to refurbish the adjacent premises so as to provide catering and other facilities within the character of the Old Swan Inn and to improve the premises generally. Planning permissions and building regulations consent are to be obtained as necessary. A comprehensive scheme is being prepared by the Consulting Architects and initial estimates for the scheme are in the region of £150,000.

2. **THE HISTORY**

The first record of the Old Swan Inn is a reference in Bentley's History of Dudley in 1840, but the terraced block in which it now stands was built in the 1860's. In 1932 the tenancy of the pub and brewery was granted to Frederick and Doris Pardoe and has remained in the family until now; in 1984 Doris – who had outlived her husband by 32 years – died.

A new era is therefore about to dawn for the Old Swan Inn, but one that is mindful of an illustrious past. It is intended that the report in "The Advertiser" of the 31st December 1910 will remain true: "The Olde Swan Still Swims. The Best and Purest Ales are now being sold at the old establishment known as The Olde Swan Inn, Halesowen Road, Netherton."

Extract from a share prospectus and an example of a share certificate.

The major multinationals are American-owned, for example Exxon and General Motors. European-owned MNC's include Royal Dutch Shell (Netherlands/UK) and British Petroleum (UK).

Activity 11

Obtain a copy of the annual report and accounts of a public limited company which operates in your area. From the information given try to identify:

a the range of products/interests with which the company or group is concerned,

b the number of people employed in its various activities,

c the sales turnover and profit,

d its sources of finance.

Conclusion

In this block, we have identified the existence of both public
and private sector, through an examination of where people
work. You should now be familiar with the major
organizations within the private sector and their main
characteristics.

Summary of skills

The intention of the study involved in this unit is not only to
learn facts about organizations, but also to develop skills
which will be of use in the business world. This section at the
end of each block of work is to indicate the skills areas you
should have developed during each activity.

Skills

Skill	Activities in which skill is developed
a Working with others	1, 7, 8
b Numeracy	1, 2, 5, 10
c Learning and studying	All activities
d Information gathering	1, 4, 5, 7, 8, 9, 10
e Communicating	2, 7, 8, 9, 10
f Design and visual discrimination	2
g Identifying and tackling problems	9

Links with other units

You should also appreciate the links which exist between
your studies in this area and your studies of *People in
Organizations* and *Finance*. These activities are related to the
understanding of organizational structures which you will
examine as part of the *People in Organizations* unit. In the
Finance unit you will develop a fuller understanding of the
internal and external sources of finance available to the
private sector and the methods used to forecast and control
expenditure.

Block 3
Organizations and the Public Sector

Introduction

This block examines in detail the various public-sector organizations which exist in our economy. Every day we all consume goods and services provided by these organizations, eg in the areas of transport, education, health, electricity, gas, etc. We will look at the range of services provided by public corporations, nationalized industries, central government and local government, and at the structure of these organizations and their financing.

| Activity 1 | Using your own knowledge and experience, try to think of as many services as possible which you consume individually and/or which are consumed by business organizations, but which are provided by a public corporation or nationalized industry, a central government department or the local authority. You could draw up a table as shown below to organize your information. |

Description of service	Provided by		
	Central government department	Local authority	Public corporation/ Nationalized industry
Refuse collection	✓	*Department of Technical Services*	✓

The work which you undertake in the rest of this block should indicate to you how accurate you have been in compiling your table.

Organizations in the public sector are all publicly owned; in reality that means owned by the state rather than by private individuals. Some of these organizations operate commercially, producing goods and/or services for sale to other organizations and the general public. In other areas the services provided by the public sector are not charged for at the time of consumption but are paid for nationally or locally with the revenue from taxation, eg state education.

We now need to go on to examine in more detail the different organizations which make up the public sector. Public corporations have been established as an alternative to central government departments and local government authorities as a means of managing certain public activities.

Public corporations

Public corporations have been defined as public trading companies created by the central government but, to a large extent, financially independent of them. Their main features are:

1 *Ownership* The State is the owner.
2 *Control* The Government appoints a board of management.
3 *Aims* To act in the public interest, making sufficient profits to cover costs.
4 *Finance* To be provided out of profits or by government loans or external borrowing.

Public corporations are generally free to manage their own affairs without detailed supervision by Parliament. However, there is intervention by government in many aspects of the operation of the corporations, e.g. government sets limits on the amount of borrowing which they can do from sources other than the government itself. These are known as **external financing limits**, (EFL's).

Nationalized industries

Public corporations include the nationalized industries. Broadly these are the industries responsible for providing energy, steel, shipbuilding, transport and postal services.

Some of the best-known nationalized industries include:

British Coal,
the British Steel Corporation,
the Post Office,
British Rail.

Most nationalized industries were created as a result of the compulsory purchase by the government of the assets and ownership of companies previously privately owned. Most of the nationalization acts which transferred the ownership of these various industries from private hands to the public sector were passed by the post-war Labour Government. There have always been a variety of arguments put forward to justify nationalization. These arguments can be listed under different headings as follows:

Natural monopolies

A monopoly is created when the supply and control of a product or service is in the hands of a single organization. It becomes a natural monopoly when it would be wasteful for more than one organization to operate, eg if there were several organizations producing electricity, there would be a needless duplication of expensive generating equipment, in contrast to a situation where a single organization could build larger and more efficient power stations. In the supply of electricity, the argument is that in private hands, this monopoly might not be operated in the best interests of the public. For instance, with no competition, artificially high prices could be charged. Nationalization may therefore be a way of protecting the public from the possible dangers of monopoly power.

Capital investment

Capital is the wealth and resources required by an industry in order to operate efficiently. Where the private sector has been either unwilling or unable to provide the large amount of capital needed to reorganize and modernize such capital-intensive industries as coal mining and the railways, the government has taken over.

Strategic industries

The products of some industries are of vital importance to the whole economy, eg iron and steel, and energy. It is argued that such essential industries should not, therefore, be looked on as sources for private profit but should be run by the State in the general interest of the nation.

Social costs and benefits

Private industry may not always take into account the side-effects of its activities, such as road congestion and pollution of the environment: these become costs to the community. Nationalized industries can consider and try to prevent these side effects.

Nationalized industries can also bring positive benefits. No private concern would operate a railway service that made a financial loss. However, British Rail does just this on some of its lines. If it did not, then some communities would become isolated.

Political conflicts

Public ownership is a central theme in the policies of the Labour Party. The Conservative Party, on the other hand, prefers private ownership of business.

In recent years since the election of a Conservative Government in 1979, opposition to, and criticism of, nationalization has grown. Some of the arguments against nationalization can be summed up as follows:

Lack of competition Nationalization means a certain amount of government control and regulation. Similar organizations cannot be set up, so the competition necessary to encourage efficiency is missing.

Freedom of choice Many of the nationalized industries are monopolies, thus limiting the individual's freedom of choice. For example, we may choose between gas, electricity, coal or oil to run a central heating system but, having chosen gas, we can only obtain a supply from one source.

Finance In the past some of the nationalized industries have been heavily subsidized by government funds. Some argue that this places a heavy burden on the tax payer.

Investment Because the nationalized industries are not bound to make a profit in order to remain in business, unwise investment decisions have been made.

Such criticisms of public ownership have been very common under both Conservative administrations since 1979. A major policy pursued by the Conservatives has been **privatization**. This is the process of putting back into the private sector concerns that were previously part of the public sector. This process has been pursued with nationalized industries, notably the sale of shares in British Telecom. It has also been advocated in other parts of the public sector, for example the sale of council houses, privatization of refuse collection services, and cleaning services in National Health Service hospitals.

The Conservative Government has made privatization a major policy because it believes that the private sector provides greater choice for consumers, greater efficiency, and lower costs.

Many other activities in the public sector are co-ordinated and provided by central government departments. The various departments of central government are headed by politicians who are appointed as Ministers, and staffed by Civil Servants who remain in their jobs irrespective of changes of government.

			Thousands
	1979	1984	1988
Civil departments			
Agriculture, Fisheries and Food	14.5	12.1	11.8
Chancellor of the Exchequer's departments			
Customs and Excise	28.8	25.1	24.7
Inland Revenue	84.6	69.8	62.9
Department for National Savings	10.8	8.0	7.6
Treasury and others	4.0	9.5	9.0
Education and Science	3.7	2.4	2.4
Employment Group	53.6	56.4	54.1
Energy	1.3	1.1	1.0
Environment (including PSA)	56.0	36.6	34.5
Foreign and Commonwealth	12.1	10.0	10.5
Health and Social Services	100.9	92.6	90.0
Home	33.5	36.4	41.1
Scotland	13.7	12.8	12.8
Trade and Industry	19.1	14.7	14.9
Transport	13.9	14.2	14.2
Welsh Office	2.6	2.2	2.2
Other civil departments	31.4	20.9	21.5
Total civil departments	484.6	424.8	415.2
Royal Ordnance Factories	23.0	18.0	
Defence	224.7	181.2	170.0
Total all departments	732.3	624.0	592.7
Of which:			
Non-industrial staff	565.8	504.3	
Industrial staff	166.5	119.7	

Civil service staff, by ministerial responsibility. (Source: Social Trends 1985)

Activity 2 Now examine the table on the previous page which gives information on people in employment within Government departments. Taking each of the departments listed, note down some examples of the specific responsibilities of those departments. In addition note which departments require the most manpower.

When you have completed your list read the section below which provides more information on the activities of government departments. You can check your list against it.

The following section shows the major government departments and their responsibilities. Most of these services or activities are centrally co-ordinated but they may be organized locally by the local authority. A good example of this is education. This is nationally the responsibility of the Department of Education and Science but the local authority administers and maintains the schools and colleges in its area.

The major government departments

Department	Main responsibilities
Agriculture, Fisheries and Food	Agriculture, horticulture, food and fishing industries. Control of animal and plant diseases. Safety and quality of food and food supply.
The Treasury	Primary responsibility for developing Britain's overall economic strategy. Control of public expenditure, responsibility for balance of payments policies. Responsibility for the preparation of economic forecasts.
Education and Science	Promotion of all forms of education throughout England, including primary, secondary, further and higher education. Links with local authorities in this provision

and bodies such as the University Grants Committee and the Research Councils.

Employment

Employment policy and industrial relations are the major areas of responsibility. The department pays unemployment benefit and links with the Manpower Services Commission and bodies such as the Advisory Conciliation and Arbitration Service and the Health and Safety Executive.

Energy

Energy supply, usage and conservation. Coal, gas, electricity industries. Atomic energy and offshore gas and oil sources. The department naturally has links with major energy suppliers, eg the CEGB (Central Electricity Generating Board) and its area boards, and the Atomic Energy Authority.

Foreign and Commonwealth

Covers all aspects of external affairs including the development of foreign policy, negotiations with other countries, and the protection of British interests abroad.

Health and Social Security

Responsible for the administration of the NHS, public health and local authority personal social services. The department is responsible for the payment of social security benefits. It has links with local authority social services departments and Regional and Area Health Authorities.

Trade and Industry	Responsible for general industrial policy including financial assistance to industry. Also has close links with some of the nationalized industries, eg the British Steel Corporation. On the trade side, activities include commercial relations with overseas countries, and administration of tariffs and export services.
Transport	Responsibility for the transport industry, railways, buses, freight and ports. Planning and construction of motorways and trunk roads. Road and vehicle safety, and vehicle and driver licensing.
Welsh Office	Assumes overall responsibility for many activities in Wales including housing, health, childcare, primary and secondary education, town and country planning.

The work of the central government departments and wide range of services provided must be funded from the revenue which government raises. By examining information given by the Central Statistical Office it should be possible to identify the major sources of income.

Activity 3

The table opposite provides figures for central government income from a variety of sources 1961–1983.
a Identify which source of income provides the largest funds for central government.
b How has the importance of the different sources changed over the period 1961–1983?

Central government finance

Central government raises revenue by levying taxes from individuals and business organizations. The table opposite

Percentages and £s million

	1961	1971	1976	1980	1981	1982	1983	1983 (£s million)
Central government *(percentages)*								
Taxes on income								
Paid by persons[1]	27.9	32.4	32.8	26.5	26.1	26.5	24.6	31,151
Paid by corporations[2]	10.7	7.4	4.5	7.3	8.2	9.2	9.5	11,978
Taxes on expenditure								
Customs and Excise duties (including VAT)	32.0	26.6	21.0	24.3	24.0	25.4	25.1	31,720
Other indirect taxes	3.2	6.5	2.4	6.3	6.3	5.5	4.5	5,689
National insurance and national health contributions								
Paid by employees	7.2	6.8	6.6	6.2	6.7	7.6	7.9	10,011
Paid by employers[3]	6.3	7.2	10.0	9.1	8.5	8.4	8.4	10,632
Rent, interest, dividends, royalties,								
and other current income	6.7	7.8	6.8	7.2	7.2	7.6	6.8	8,653
Taxes on capital[4]	3.3	3.3	1.6	1.2	1.4	1.3	1.2	1,482
Borrowing requirement	2.9	3.2	13.3	11.8	9.9	6.9	11.4	14,462
Other income	−0.2	−1.2	1.0	0.1	1.7	1.6	0.6	697
Total (=100%) (£s million)	7,941	20,094	50,824	91,338	104,627	113,370	126,475	126,475
Local authorities *(percentages)*								
Current grants from central government								
Rate support grants and other non-specific grants	23.3	33.3	41.2	35.0	38.6	38.6	34.4	13,123
Specific grants	7.3	3.7	8.0	8.6	8.7	9.7	14.1	5,372
Total current grants from central government	30.6	37.0	49.2	43.6	47.3	48.3	48.5	18,495
Rates	30.8	27.0	24.0	27.4	32.5	35.9	32.6	12,456
Rent	9.3	9.1	9.6	10.0	10.2	9.5	7.8	2,961
Interest, dividends, and other current income	7.2	6.3	6.4	6.7	6.8	7.0	6.2	2,369
Capital grants from central government	1.7	2.2	0.9	1.1	1.1	1.1	1.0	381
Borrowing requirement	17.6	17.8	8.7	9.8	0.9	−2.3	3.3	1,253
Other income	2.8	0.6	1.2	1.4	1.2	0.5	0.6	214
Total (=100%) (£s million)	2,702	7,724	18,782	30,265	31,982	33,320	38,135	38,135
Total general government income (excluding intra-sector transactions) (£s million)	9,725	23,477	58,643	104,110	116,966	128,489	138,306	138,306

[1] Including surtax.
[2] Including profits tax and overspill relief.
[3] Including employers' contributions to the redundancy fund.
[4] Death duties, capital transfer tax, capital gains tax, and development land tax. Includes also other capital receipts.

Central government and local authority income, by source. (Source: Social Trends 1985)

indicates that in 1961 Customs and Excise duties provided 32 per cent of government income but between 1971 and 1982 personal income taxes provided the largest source of revenue. The changes shown by the table include the fact that taxes on expenditure accounted for a growing proportion of central government income between 1976 and 1980 (from 23 to 31 per cent) but have remained at 30 per cent of income since then. Taxes on expenditure are taxes levied on spending on goods and services, as opposed to taxes on income which are levied on all types of earnings made by individuals and organizations.

The table on central government funds also shows that the proportion of income raised from personal income taxes fell from 33 per cent in 1976 to 25 per cent in 1983. Central government also raises income by borrowing and this borrowing requirement fell sharply from 13 per cent in 1979 to 7 per cent in 1982, but rose again in 1983 to 11 per cent.

It is possible to break down the various sources of government revenue further. *Taxes on income*, *Taxes on expenditure*, and *Taxes on capital* are general headings which include a number of different types of taxes.

Taxes on income

These taxes are collected by the Inland Revenue and include **Income tax** which is levied on individuals' income, and **Corporation tax** which is levied on the gross profits of companies.

Taxes on expenditure

These taxes include **Customs and Excise duties**, **Value Added Tax** and a variety of other **indirect taxes**, eg gambling, motor vehicle duty, etc.

Taxes on capital

These are taxes which are levied on the ownership or transfer of assets, eg property, shares in companies. They include **Capital gains tax** and **Inheritance tax.**

The table below gives some detail on these various taxes and duties.

Sources of finance for central government

Tax/Duty	Description
Income tax	Income tax is a direct tax, it is paid directly to the government by the taxpayer or their employer. It is paid on both earned income (wages and salaries) and on unearned income (rent from property, dividends on shares, etc) and is a progressive tax, ie the higher the earnings, the more tax is paid as a proportion of those earnings. It is not chargeable on the whole of a person's income since a variety of allowances reduce the amount of taxable income. (You will examine this in greater detail when covering personal finance in the *Finance* unit).

Value Added
Tax (VAT)

This is a tax on the value of goods and services, added progressively throughout the various stages of production. It is a general sales tax and is charged to all sellers of all products and services. Each seller is able to deduct the VAT which they have paid on their supplies and so must pay tax only on 'the value added' to the product. Therefore the producers of intermediate components or products only pay tax on the value of the work they perform. The final consumer bears the full burden of the tax as it is passed on in the form of higher final prices.

Most products or services are subject to VAT but certain goods and services are given special treatment and are exempt or zero rated. When goods and services are exempt, the trader does not charge the customer any output tax but cannot claim back any VAT already paid on inputs. Insurance, betting, education and health services are just some examples of areas where exemption applies. Zero-rating means complete relief from VAT. A trader does not charge VAT on goods and services sold and any VAT paid on inputs can be reclaimed. Examples of zero-rated goods and services include food (except meals out), books, newspapers, transport and children's clothing. A major reason for the introduction of VAT in the United Kingdom was that it is a necessary condition of membership of the European Economic Community (EEC).

Corporation tax

This is a tax levied on the profits of companies. Dividends paid to individual shareholders are taxed through personal income tax but it is assumed that the basic rate of income tax has been applied to dividends before they are paid out (part of the corporation tax paid by a company is imputed to its shareholders). The remainder of a company's profit is taxed through corporation tax at a standard rate. The tax rate has been reduced substantially over recent years and is now 35 per cent; small companies pay a reduced rate of 29 per cent. Corporation tax may encourage firms to raise funds in the form of loan capital, eg debentures, rather than by an issue of shares, because interest on loan capital can be offset against corporation tax as a cost of production, whereas dividends cannot.

Customs and
Excise duties

Customs duties are duties levied on goods imported from abroad. Excise duties are taxes on certain goods produced in this country. Most of the revenue from excise duties is derived from three sources: tobacco, alcoholic drinks and hydrocarbon oil (petrol and diesel fuel). The government can raise taxes on these commodities without prompting a significant fall in sales (and so in tax revenue). This is because demand for these products is relatively inelastic, ie demand is unresponsive to a change in price—the government can raise taxes on these products and people will continue to buy them even at the higher price.

Capital gains tax

This tax is levied on the profit made by an organization or an individual on the purchase and then resale of certain items of capital. A capital gain is the difference between the price at which something is bought and the (higher) price at which it is later sold. The tax is levied on this gain, eg if you bought 100 shares at £1 per share and later sold them for £2 per share then your capital gain would be £100 and would therefore be subject to tax.

Inheritance tax

This tax replaced *capital transfer tax* in the 1986 budget. Capital transfer tax was a tax on the transfer of wealth from one individual to another and was payable whether the transfer took place while the benefactor (the person giving the gift) was alive or upon their death. Inheritance tax is concerned with the taxation of wealth when it is transferred upon a person's death. The 1986 budget abolished capital transfer tax on lifetime gifts between individuals and renamed the tax as Inheritance tax.

Petroleum revenue tax

This tax is levied on the net revenue from oil and gas fields. Net revenue comprises the receipts from the sale of oil and gas, less royalties (also paid to the government) and operating costs (excluding interest payments).

Stamp duty

This duty is payable on certain legal and commercial documents. Among the more common of these documents are the ones connected with the transfer of ownership of land and buildings.

Other duties	These include a variety of duties levied and include: *Car tax* This is a special tax on motor cars and motor caravans, levied in addition to VAT. *Motor vehicle excise duty* All vehicles in use in the UK must be registered and licensed. The rates of duty payable vary according to the type of vehicle. *Licences* Central government obtains revenue from the issue of a variety of licences, eg television licences.
National Insurance	National Insurance contributions are paid by both employees and their employers and provide revenue for the payment of benefits under the national insurance scheme. You will examine this in greater detail when looking at personal finance in the *Finance* unit.

Government borrowing

We have seen that government raises a great deal of revenue through taxation. However, most governments have found that their expenditure exceeds their expected revenue and they therefore have to borrow in order to finance their level of spending. The annual difference between spending and income levels is known as the **Public Sector Borrowing Requirement** (PSBR). This is made up of the borrowing needs of central government, local government and public corporations.

There are a number of different ways in which central government can borrow. These methods of borrowing can be divided into two broad areas: marketable and nonmarketable debts.

Marketable debt

The government, through the Bank of England (which acts as the government's banker), issues **treasury bills** and

government securities (also known as gilt-edged securities) in order to obtain funds. Organizations such as banks, pension funds, building societies, insurance companies and other commercial organizations will buy bills and securities.

THIS FORM MAY BE USED

TENDER FORM

This form must be lodged at the Bank of England, New Issues (I), Watling Street, London, EC4M 9AA not later than 10.00 A.M. ON THURSDAY, 29TH MAY 1986, or at any of the Branches of the Bank of England or at the Glasgow Agency of the Bank of England not later than 3.30 P.M. ON WEDNESDAY, 28TH MAY 1986.

ISSUE BY TENDER OF £400,000,000

3 per cent Treasury Stock, 1991

MINIMUM TENDER PRICE £86.00 PER CENT

TO THE GOVERNOR AND COMPANY OF THE BANK OF ENGLAND

I/We tender in accordance with the terms of the prospectus dated 23rd May 1986 as follows:—

Amount of above-mentioned Stock tendered for, being a minimum of £100 and in a multiple as follows:—

Amount of Stock tendered for	Multiple
£100—£1,000	£100
£1,000—£3,000	£500
£3,000—£10,000	£1,000
£10,000—£50,000	£5,000
£50,000 or greater	£25,000

1. NOMINAL AMOUNT OF STOCK

£

Sum enclosed, being the amount required for payment in full, i.e. the price tendered (minimum of £86.00) for every £100 of the nominal amount of Stock tendered for (shown in Box 1 above):—

2. AMOUNT OF PAYMENT *(a)*

£

The price tendered per £100 Stock, being a multiple of 25p and not less than the minimum tender price of £86.00:—

3. TENDER PRICE *(b)*

£ : p

I/We request that any letter of allotment in respect of Stock allotted to me/us be sent by post at my/our risk to me/us at the address shown below.

.... **May 1986**

SIGNATURE..
of, or on behalf of, tenderer

PLEASE USE BLOCK CAPITALS

MR/MRS MISS	FORENAME(S) IN FULL	SURNAME

FULL POSTAL ADDRESS:—			
POST-TOWN	COUNTY	POSTCODE	

Advertisement for Treasury Stock.

Treasury bills These are loans to the government, usually with a life of 91 days; they therefore supply government's short-term borrowing needs. Each week the government borrows large sums of money by offering Treasury bills for sale. They do not carry a fixed rate of interest. Each week various financial institutions submit bids for the following week's offer of Treasury bills. The government accepts the highest bid made: the higher the bid price, the lower the rate of interest which the government has to pay for its borrowed funds. Treasury bills are marketable as they can be resold by the holder to a third party at any time prior to repayment by the government (ie maturity).

Gilt-edged securities These are government stock sold to individuals, organizations and financial institutions. The government promises to pay a fixed rate of interest for a number of years and then repay the original sum. Gilts are marketable and are often sold and resold many times. The holder of the security at the time of maturity receives not only the interest for that year, but also repayment of the initial sum.

Nonmarketable debt

Individuals purchase premium bonds and national savings certificates and in doing so are lending money to government. The individual receives interest on the loan and repayment of the sum on maturity. The term nonmarketable debt is used because such bonds and certificates cannot be transferred or sold to others.

Local authorities

The other major area covering the public provision of goods and services is local authority activity. As we have already seen when examining the responsibilities of central government departments, many of these are linked to the provision of services by local authorities. In order to begin to identify some of the main activities of local authorities, we can examine the areas which provide employment within local government.

| *Activity 4* | The following table provides figures for local authority manpower broken down by services. Using the figures |

for 1984, rank the services in order, from those requiring the greatest manpower to those requiring the least.

			Thousands
	1979	1983	1984
Education—lecturers and teachers	638.5	611.5	608.6
—others	472.9	428.1	424.8
Construction	155.9	137.2	132.9
Transport	31.4	28.1	27.7
Social services	233.0	245.5	251.4
Public libraries and museums	36.6	36.5	37.0
Recreation, parks, and baths	84.9	86.4	87.0
Environmental health	23.9	23.2	23.4
Refuse collection and disposal	60.3	53.0	51.0
Housing	53.5	59.0	62.2
Town and country planning	23.5	22.7	23.0
Fire service—regular	39.0	40.1	40.5
—others	5.9	5.7	5.7
Miscellaneous services	300.0	286.2	288.5
Police—all ranks	123.0	134.1	134.5
—cadets	3.9	1.4	1.0
—civilians	38.4	40.6	41.1
—traffic wardens	5.2	5.3	5.5
Agency staff	0.5	0.6	0.6
Magistrates' courts/district courts	8.1	9.1	9.3
Probation—officers	5.0	5.8	5.9
—others	4.2	5.4	5.7
Total	2,347.7	2,265.7	2,267.4

Local authority manpower, by service.

The table shows that Education, Miscellaneous Services, Social Services, the Police, Recreation, Parks and Baths, and Housing, are the major areas of employment for which local authorities have responsibility.

The local government system consists of elected councils and their permanent (nonelected) staff, each representing a local area. Each council, dependent upon size, provides a range of services from education to refuse collection.

Local government in Britain was reorganized in 1974 to provide the two-tier structure shown below.

The structure of local government.

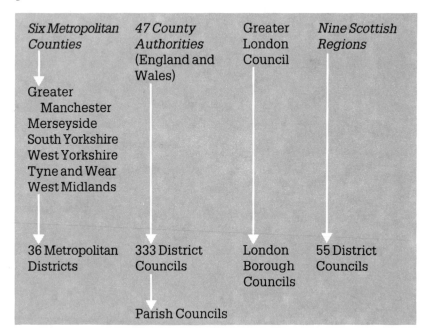

Six Metropolitan Counties	47 County Authorities (England and Wales)	Greater London Council	Nine Scottish Regions
Greater Manchester Merseyside South Yorkshire West Yorkshire Tyne and Wear West Midlands			
36 Metropolitan Districts	333 District Councils	London Borough Councils	55 District Councils
	Parish Councils		

Structure of local government

A great deal of the country is administered by the county authorities, eg Nottinghamshire and Essex. These county councils usually provide the large-scale services in their area, eg education. Within each county area there will also be a number of district authorities which are responsible for the more localized services, eg refuse collection. Below these are parish councils which provide minor local amenities such as sports facilities and village halls.

The 1974 reorganization of local government recognized the existence in England of heavily populated areas or conurbations. In these areas local authority responsibilities were split between the Metropolitan County Council and the Metropolitan District Council. On the 1 April 1986, the Metropolitan County Councils and the Greater London Council were abolished. The responsibilities which they previously held have now either been taken over by the District Councils in the area or are administered by new bodies called Joint Boards.

Local Authority responsibilities

<table>
<tr><td>

Activity 5

</td><td>

Find out the name of your district and county authority (if applicable) and the following details about them.
a The size of population.
b The other district councils within the county.
c The political composition of the council.

The best source for this type of information is *The Municipal Yearbook* which should be available in your library.

</td></tr>
</table>

Responsibility for the provision of public services in any area will be split between the district and county authority and also the local Regional Health Authority and the local Water Authority. The district and county authorities provide a wide range of services from education to road repairs.

Local authority services

One of the best ways of finding out the services provided by your local district and county authority is to look at the information provided by the local council to accompany the rate demand to households. In order to finance some of their services local authorities can tax locally by the levy of rates. Every household pays rates each year. Accompanying the rate bill there is usually a leaflet explaining where the local authority obtains its funds and how it intends to spend them.

<table>
<tr><td>

Activity 6

</td><td>

Obtain a copy of the rate precept information provided by your local county council or district council. Look at the expenditure on all the services provided and identify the five largest expenditure areas. Make notes detailing the specific services provided under the five headings.

</td></tr>
</table>

An example of the sort of information provided by Nottinghamshire County Council is provided on the next page. From the table given, we can identify the following five main areas of expenditure: Education, Social Services, Police, Road Improvements and Maintenance, and Fire.

The information which you have obtained from your own district or county authority should provide you with an idea of the range of public services available. Some of these

Analysis of expenditure and income on services

The estimated gross expenditure and income on the various services for 1985-86 and 1986-87 is shown in the following tables. A contingency provision of £14 million is included in 1986-87 which, together with a further £16 million being held within the Council's reserves, will be used primarily to meet the cost of pay awards.

	1985-86			1986-87		
	Gross Expenditure £m	Income £m	Net Expenditure £m	Gross Expenditure £m	Income £m	Net Expenditure £m
Education	280.1	41.0	239.1	290.9	47.4	243.5
Road Improvements and Maintenance	33.6	5.6	28.0	35.6	7.4	28.2
Transportation	8.3	1.3	7.0	8.3	1.3	7.0
Other Environmental Services	5.7	0.4	5.3	6.0	0.5	5.5
Libraries	7.8	0.5	7.3	8.2	0.6	7.6
Other Leisure Services	7.9	1.2	6.7	8.3	1.3	7.0
Police	51.3	27.8	23.5	55.5	29.9	25.6
Economic Development, Community Programme, etc.	4.3	2.8	1.5	4.7	3.2	1.5
Fire	12.1	0.8	11.3	12.5	1.0	11.5
Trading Standards, Registrars	2.7	0.9	1.8	2.9	1.0	1.9
Social Services	62.3	9.8	52.5	68.1	10.2	57.9
Probation and Magistrates' Courts	7.3	5.9	1.4	7.7	6.1	1.6
East Midlands Airport	0.6	1.3	0.7(−)	0.6	0.9	0.3(−)
Other	7.7	5.4	2.3	7.7	5.2	2.5
	491.7	104.7	387.0	517.0	116.0	401.0
Contingency	16.2	−	16.2	14.0	−	14.0
	507.9	104.7	403.2	531.0	116.0	415.0

Extract from Nottinghamshire County Council rate precept.

services are provided solely by either the district authority or the county authority; responsibility for others is shared. The responsibility taken for services in the nonmetropolitan areas is shown in the table opposite, eg Town and Country Planning is one of the functions which is shared between the district and county council.

Local government responsibility for services

Since the abolition of the Greater London Council and the Metropolitan Counties the functions which these bodies previously carried out have been redistributed. Joint Boards have been set up to oversee the provision of police, fire and

Local government responsibility for services

Responsibility	County Council	District Council
Clean Air		✓
Environmental Health	✓	
Town & Country Planning	✓	✓
Transport & Highways	✓	✓
Education	✓	
Libraries	✓	
Museums & Art Galleries	✓	✓
Consumer Protection	✓	
Youth Employment	✓	
Housing		✓
Personal Social Services	✓	
Parks, Recreation	✓	✓
Refuse Collection		✓
Refuse Disposal	✓	
Sewerage (local servicing)		✓
Fire and Police	✓	

public transport. The London Borough Councils and the Metropolitan District Councils have taken over responsibility for most of the other services, including highways, traffic management, waste regulation and disposal, trading standards, arts, sports and leisure.

We have already seen that local authorities provide a wide variety of public services. These services cost money and the authorities must obtain finance from a variety of sources in order to be able to fund them.

Activity 7	Using the copy of the rate precept information which you have obtained from your local district or county council, examine the information provided on sources of income. Identify the major sources of income for your council.

The main sources of income for local authorities are given below.

1 *Central government grants*

Much of local authority current expenditure (eg, spending on wages as opposed to capital expenditure on buildings) is funded by finance from central government, which calculates how much is needed by local authorities to provide their services. It is then decided what percentage of this shall be provided by means of central government grants. The grants are then distributed to individual local authorities.

Government grants make up about half of the revenue of local authorities and are provided for a number of reasons:

a To offset the disadvantages of the rating system by transferring part of the burden to general taxation.
b To ensure a minimum standard of provision for certain services.
c To assist local authorities with the provision of services of national concern, police, education, roads.

Central government provides local authorities with two main types of grant. Firstly, specific grants which local authorities have to use on specified services, eg the police: obviously these can be used by central government to ensure that certain minimum standards are maintained. Secondly, central government provides the Rate Support Grant (RSG), which is a block grant to assist with the wide range of services which local authorities provide. It is calculated on a formula which takes into account the rate resources available to the authority, the density of population and the make up of the population, eg the numbers of young and old people within an area.

In recent years it has been government policy to shift more of the cost of local services onto rates and away from other forms of taxation. This has affected all local authorities and, as the Secretary of State for the Environment told the House of Commons on the 24 July 1984 it '. . . continues the trend we have set over recent years of shifting the burden of local authority expenditure away from the taxpayer and towards the ratepayer, thereby increasing local authorities' accountability to the electorate . . .'.

2 Rates

Rates are a tax on property, ie houses, shops, offices and factories. Unlike most other taxes they are not raised by central government but by local authorities.

Each property within a local authority's area is given a rateable value and the larger the property the higher its rateable value will be. The rateable value of property is determined by the Valuation Officer of the Inland Revenue. If structural alterations are made to a property then the rateable value may be amended. If an authority adds up all the rateable values of the properties in its area, then that is the Total Rateable Value (TRV) of that area.

Each year every local council decides how much, in total, it needs to raise through the rates. The authority will do this once it knows how much income it will obtain from other sources. Assume that an authority wishes to raise £246 million through the rates. It must then calculate the rate poundage, ie the amount of money per pound of rateable value to be paid by the ratepayers. It does this as follows:

$$\frac{\textbf{Amount required from rates}}{\textbf{Total rateable value}} = \frac{\textbf{£246 m.}}{\textbf{£138 m.}} = \textbf{1.78}$$

Therefore the rate poundage = 178p in £1

Having calculated its rate poundage, the local authority can now send out its rate demand to property owners. Assume that a property has been given a rateable value of £200. The rate poundage had been set at 178p in the pound, therefore the rates payable will be

$$£200 \times 178p = £356 \text{ per year.}$$

Rates then, are the method by which the local community pays its share for the services provided by the local authorities—the county council, the borough council and, in some areas, the parish council. The amount of rates depends on the spending levels of the councils. Each council reaches its own decision on this and the rates are then added together and collected by the District Council on behalf of them all.

3 Charges for services

Users of some public services may make some payment when they use them, for example council house rents, admission fees to leisure centres, civic theatres, etc. This forms part of the local authorities' income.

4 *Borrowing*

Local authorities usually borrow money for large-scale capital projects, such as the purchase of building land for housing. Such borrowing is subject to permission from the Department of the Environment. Authorities may borrow from central government or from the private sector by borrowing from banks or other financial institutions.

5 *Reserves*

Councils have a large money turnover through all their activities and therefore hold substantial reserves to ensure that they can always meet their obligations. For example they will have to pay bills, salaries and wages while awaiting the receipt of grants, rates, rents, etc. Some councils may decide actually to use up some of their reserves to pay for services, but of course they cannot do this indefinitely or they will exhaust the reserves.

You should now have a clear idea of the extent of local authority services and the various ways in which those services are financed. The activities which you have already undertaken in this block will help you to compare information from two different county authorities. This information begins opposite on page 77 and there are relevant activities on pages 79–80. This work will conclude your examination of public sector organizations and their structures and functions.

Essex and Cheshire rate precept and Municipal Yearbook extracts.

Essex County Council

Facts behind the COUNTY RATE 1985/86

151·5p
increase of 7·45%
(about 50p per householder per week)

Primary Schools	Secondary Schools
Special Education	School Meals
Colleges	Adult Education
Careers Service	Youth and Community Services
Country Parks	Smallholdings
Fire Brigade	Emergency Planning
Highways	Consumer Protection
Street Lighting	Refuse Disposal
Libraries	County Archives
Magistrates' Courts	Probation
Planning	Economic Promotion
Police	School Crossing Patrols
Care of Elderly	Care of Children
Home Helps	Meals on Wheels
Care of Handicapped	Aids to Physically Handicapped

YOUR RATE IS UP — WHY?

The rate precept is increasing by more than inflation as a result of the Government's policy of reducing grant. At 151.5p the rate precept has increased by 10.5p or 7.45%. After taking into account inflation, the Government's Grant is being reduced by the equivalent of a 6p rate rise (4.3%.) This reduction of grant occurs despite the Council having set its budget at the Government's 1985/86 target level. This target is some £24M less than the Government's assessment of the amount needed to provide a standard level of service in Essex. If expenditure had been set above the target level, severe grant penalties would have been incurred.

Expenditure cuts have been avoided but more efficient working methods are being introduced. Service priorities are under constant review and some improvements have been made.

To keep within the target less capital expenditure will be financed from internal funds, and reserves will be used.

	p in £	Cost to ratepayers £M
The County rate in 1984/85 was –	141.00*	332.4*
Inflation (less grant) –	8.34	19.7
Loss of Rate Support Grant –	6.07	14.3
Loss of Transport Supplementary Grant –	1.41	3.3
Increase in service expenditure –	2.78	6.5
	159.60	376.2
Capital financing policy changes and use of reserves and balances –	– 6.82	– 16.0
Increased rateable values –	– 1.28	—
1985/86 COUNTY RATE	151.50*	360.2*

This rate is collected by District Councils on behalf of the County.

*The figures reflect a Metropolitan Police adjustment within the Epping Forest District.

HOW IS THE MONEY SPENT?

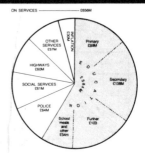

ON SERVICES — £656M

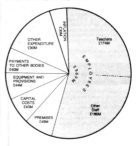

ON RUNNING COSTS (STAFF ETC.) – £656M

WHERE DOES THE COUNTY'S MONEY COME FROM?

TOTAL INCOME OF £656M IS PROVIDED AS FOLLOWS:

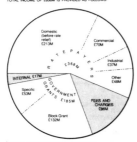

"Internal" includes the use of reserves and balances.

INFLATION AND RESERVES

A provision for inflation of £30M, in line with current inflation trends, has been included in the estimates. With regard to reserves, the County Fund balance is estimated to fall from £14.1M to £6.3M during the year (from 2.6% to 1.1% of net expenditure). The General Reserve is estimated to fall from £14.3M to £5.0M after making a provision for possible emergency expenditure.

RATE INCOME AND RATEABLE VALUES

Rateable Values of properties in Essex, at 1 April 1984, were:

	£M	% of total
Domestic	139.4	58
Commercial	46.7	19
Industrial	24.0	10
Other	31.3	13
TOTAL	241.4	100

A 1p County Council rate is estimated to raise £2.385M.

MANPOWER LEVELS

The table below analyses the number of staff provided for in the budget. Totals are for whole-time equivalent staff (that is, part-time staff are converted to full-time according to the number of hours worked).

Numbers employed by each County service:

	1984/85	1985/86
EDUCATION	22,097	21,795
SOCIAL SERVICES	4,883	5,282
POLICE	3,605	3,634
FIRE AND PUBLIC PROTECTION	1,158	1,170
LIBRARIES	710	709
HIGHWAYS	532	547
DIRECT LABOUR ORGANISATIONS	212	216
ESTATES AND ARCHITECTS	428	434
TREASURERS	405	410
SUPPLIES	326	325
CHIEF EXECUTIVE AND CLERKS	227	243
PLANNING	137	140
OTHER SERVICES	361	371
TOTAL	35,081	35,276

"Other Services" include Magistrates' Courts, Registrars of Births, Marriages and Deaths, and Rent Officers.

The Direct Labour Organisations deal mainly with Highways repair work.

Some part-time employees working very few hours have been excluded from the table. Their numbers have increased from 3,548 to 3,588.

"Whole time equivalent" employees have increased by 195 (0.6%).

CAPITAL PROGRAMME

The 1985/86 capital programme again gives emphasis to the road programme and expenditure on schools. A start is to be made on the Writtle bypass, 9 major school projects including the Colchester secondary rationalisation scheme, a major expansion of Chelmsford's further education facilities and the second phase of County Hall redevelopment including a new library.

	£M
Highways	16.6
Education	14.4
Personnel	5.8
Police	2.8
Libraries	2.4
Social Services	2.3
Fire and Public Protection	1.2
Other Services	3.1
Total Capital Expenditure	48.6

COUNTY SPENDING, THE RATE, GOVERNMENT GRANTS AND PRICES

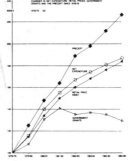

The County's net spending has risen broadly in line with inflation over the past seven years. During this period the Government has pursued a policy of shifting the burden of local authority expenditure away from the taxpayer and towards the ratepayer by reducing the proportion of expenditure met by Government grants. This policy is intended to increase local authorities' accountability to the local electorate.

Changes in the formula used to allocate Government grants between local authorities has resulted in a 16% greater loss of grant to Essex County Council than to local government as a whole.

This factor has caused the precept to increase considerably faster than prices.

FURTHER INFORMATION ON COUNTY FINANCES –

is available from the County Treasurer, County Hall, Chelmsford. The County Council Budget Book and Capital Programme for 1985/86 and the Council's Annual Report for 1983/84 are available for consultation at all branch libraries. Finance Committee and other agendas are held by most libraries. A separate publication on the County's Superannuation Fund is produced by the County Treasurer.

Printed by the Essex County Council Supplies Department   PSL 1905

© Cheshire

What we do
What it costs
Where the money comes from

1985-86

What does the County Council do and What Does it Cost?

Here is a brief summary of what the County Council is planning to spend on services, together with some key statistics.

Services	1985-86 £m
Education 76,300 pupils in primary schools; 73,000 pupils in secondary schools; 35,700 students in colleges; 595 schools and colleges; 11,900 student grants	278
Social Services 2,540 clients in homes (e.g. elderly persons, mentally handicapped, children in care); 22,000 other clients (e.g. home helps, day care centres)	49
Police 42,300 recorded crimes; 49% detection rate	43
Highways and Transportation Maintenance of 3,500 Miles of Roads; Support to bus services; Road Safety	37
Fire Brigade 10,900 Call-outs; 5,800 Fires; 13,400 Fire Prevention Inspections	12
Libraries Museums and Arts 56 Public Libraries; 11.7m Book Issues; 8 Mobile Libraries; 3 Museums; Records Office	8
Magistrates' Courts and Probation 39 Magistrates' Courts dealing with 45,400 defendants; Probation Caseload of 2,500 Clients	5
Waste Disposal 1.1m Tons of Waste	4
Planning and Environmental Services	3
Countryside and Recreation Tatton Park and 6 Country Parks; 18 Picnic Sites; 4 Walking Trails; 1 Sports Centre	2
Employment Promotion	2
Trading Standards Fair Trading and Consumer Protection	1
Other Services and Expenditure	3
Total County Council Expenditure on Services	447
Precepts Paid to Other Bodies	2
Total	**£449m**

Where does the money come from?

The following chart shows the different sources of County Council income in 1985-86.

The proportion provided by Central Government is again being reduced. This means that the ratepayer has to pay more.

Total Income £449m (from ratepayers £246m)

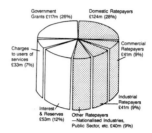

Government Grants £117m (26%)
Domestic Ratepayers £124m (28%)
Commercial Ratepayers £41m (9%)
Industrial Ratepayers £41m (9%)
Other Ratepayers —Nationalised Industries, Public Sector, etc. £40m (9%)
Interest & Reserves £53m (12%)
Charges to users of services £33m (7%)

The Reduction in Grants

Government policy is to shift more of the cost of local services onto rates and away from other forms of taxation. Nationally this transfer is equivalent to 4p off income tax since 1975.

The diagrams below show the Cheshire position today compared with 1975-76.

The Financing of Net Expenditure

1975-76 — Rate-payer / Govern-ment

During this period the ratepayer's share of each £1 spent by the Council has gone up from 37p to 71p

1985-86 — Govern-ment / Rate-payer

The Council's rate, as determined by a majority of its members, is required to maintain existing services, subject to some degree of expansion where this has been shown to be necessary and where there is a need to meet new legislative commitments, and offset by significant savings where demand for services is contracting and where the efficiency of the service has been improved.

Why has the rate increased this year?

	Rate Equivalent p
The Rate for 1984-85 was	169.0

The increase this year is explained below:

- More expenditure falls to be paid for by the ratepayer because the Government will pay less grant to the Council (9.0p of this loss is as a result of the Council spending more than the target set by the Government) — 22.3
- National pay awards and price increases — 6.8
- The Council is committed to spending more money to maintain the existing level of services, to carry through new policies begun in 1984-85, and to pay for the running costs of new capital schemes — 2.2
- New initiatives, some of which are —Improvements to the home help service —New day centres for the mentally handicapped and mentally ill —Expansion of the Probation Service —Increases in road maintenance — 2.2

Offset by:—
- Efficiency and the continuing search for economies has enabled the Council to make reductions in spending — 2.9—
- An increase in rateable resources has helped to keep the rate increase down — 1.9—
- The Council is conscious of the effect a reduction in Government grant could have on ratepayers. It has therefore decided to use money from reserves. The amount used this year is greater than in 1984-85 by — 19.7—

Increase (5.3%)	9.0
The rate for 1985-86 is	**178.0p**

The County rate is collected by each District Council with its own rate.

Rates, Grants and the Retail Prices Index

The graph below compares increases in County expenditure and the County rate with the Retail Prices Index, and shows how grants have fallen.

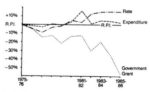

Rate
R.P.I.
Expenditure
Government Grant

+10% / R.P.I. / -10% / -20% / -30% / -40% / -50%

1975-76 / 1981-82 / 1983-84 / 1985-86

What about reserves?

Reserves are needed
—To pay bills, salaries and wages pending the receipt of rates and grants
—As a contingency in case of unexpected problems
—To assist the Council in its financing strategy and to maximise Government grant

The level in 1985-86 will be equivalent to 3.9% of the County Council's total expenditure.

How many staff does the Council employ?

There continues to be a reduction in manpower. By March 1986 numbers will have fallen by almost 3,000 in seven years.

Service	Actual March 1979	Budget March 1986
Education—teachers	11,367	10,076
other staff	8,451	6,644
Social Services	3,512	3,985
Police	2,331	2,410
Highways and Transportation	1,188	1,051
Fire Brigade	770	797
Libraries, Museums and Arts	418	427
Magistrates' Courts and Probation	308	366
Waste Disposal	95	100
Planning and Environmental Services	151	124
Countryside and Recreation	92	113
Employment Promotion	11	81
Trading Standards	59	65
Financial, legal and other professional Services	906	791
Other services	386	348
Total all services	**30,045**	**27,378**

These figures include part-time staff whose hours worked are taken as a proportion of full-time.

What new building and construction works are there in 1985-86?

The Council is planning to spend £27m on capital schemes in 1985-86. These are long term projects, where the cost to the ratepayer is spread over a number of years. Some of the main projects are:

- Extensions to Montford County High School, Warrington
- Derelict land reclamation, Foundry Lane, Widnes
- Ellesmere Port town centre traffic management scheme
- Helsby County High School extension
- Elderly person's home, Poynton
- A534 Holt-Farndon Bypass
- A5020 extension/Radway Green link
- Sports hall and student facilities, South Cheshire College of Further Education, Crewe
- Sandbach day centre for mentally handicapped

Where can I get further information?

The County Council publishes a comprehensive budget report which will be made available at libraries and information centres throughout the county.

In December 1984 the County published its annual report for the period 1983-84. The report explains what the Council does and what its priorities are, and also provides detailed information about services. It also includes the name, address and telephone number of your local County Councillor. The annual report may be obtained at a price of £1 (+50p p+p) from the County Secretary at County Hall, Chester. It is also available at libraries, as are copies of the following publications:

Cheshire Current Facts and Figures
Cheshire Facts of County Life

In addition the telephone numbers of your local County Council offices can be found in the telephone directory for your area.

Rateable values are not the responsibility of the County or District Councils. Any enquiries about the rateable value of your property should be addressed to the local Valuation Officer, whose telephone number can be found under 'Inland Revenue' in the appropriate directory.

March 1985
County Hall
Chester

ESSEX

Pop., 1,491,700; RV, £238,424,000; Rate Precept, 140·54p; Debt, £220,764,000; Area, 367,190 hectares.

Mileage of Highways: Motorway and Trunk 100; Principal 378; Classified 1,460; Unclassified 2,492.

Community Homes: 26; Schools—Nursery: 2; Primary: 601; Secondary Selective: 8; Secondary modern: 7; Secondary boarding: 2; Secondary Comprehensive: 95; Sixth form Colleges: 2; Bilateral: 2; Special: 40; Colleges of Further Education: 4; Agricultural College: 1; Institutes of Higher Education: 2; Short-term residential Adult College: 1; Technical Colleges: 3; Fire Stations: 51; Libraries—Headquarters: 1; Branch: 90; Mobile and relocatable: 18; School: 815; Elderly Persons' Homes: 63; Police Stations: 119.

Parliamentary Constituencies (16): Basildon; Billericay; Braintree; Brentwood and Ongar, Castle Point; Chelmsford; Epping Forest; Harlow; Harwich; North Colchester; Rochford; Saffron Walden; South Colchester and Maldon; Southend East; Southend West; Thurrock.

EEC Constituencies (2): Essex North East, Essex South West.

Petty Sessional Divisions: 18.

Regional Water Authorities: (1) Anglian; (2) Thames.

Audit by Arthur Andersen.

Twinning. Seine-et-Maone (France).

DISTRICT COUNCILS IN THE COUNTY

Basildon, Braintree, Brentwood, Castle Point, Chelmsford (B), Colchester (B), Epping Forest, Harlow, Maldon, Rochford, Southend-on-Sea (B), Tendring, Thurrock (B), Uttlesford.

TOPOGRAPHY

Essex is still a rapidly expanding county, where historic towns thrive alongside modern communities, such as the two new towns and the County Council's own scheme of development for South Woodham Ferrers which is now well established. One of the main reasons for this growth, both residential and industrial, is its ease of access to London; recently the opening of the M25 in Essex has given the county better communications through the national motorway network with all parts of the country and made it more attractive to developers. In addition, Essex is an important gateway to the Continent through the ports of Tilbury and Harwich and Parkeston and Southend and Stansted Airports. The ever-growing Tilbury docks handle trade with all parts of the world. Most of the industrial activity in Essex is centred on the Thames, but modern industries of many kinds can be found in or near the towns elsewhere in the county, with the more traditional industries and crafts in the rural areas. The Council has appointed an Employment Promotion

Officer in the County Planning Department responsible for economic initiatives in the planning field to attract industrial growth and a handbook "Enterprise in Essex" is available.

In contrast to industrial Thames-side the hinterland of Essex is one of the main cereal-growing areas in England and fruit-growing, market gardening and sugar beet cultivation are other important agricultural activities. The oyster farms—of historic significance—cockling and other inshore fishing still yield valuable 'crops' along the creeks and estuaries.

Essex is also a holiday county, with its north-east coast seaside resorts, the large town of Southend-on-Sea on the Thames estuary, and its riverside towns many of which have developed as yachting centres to meet the growing popularity of this form of recreation. Inland there are the attractions of several county parks and of the Epping and Hatfield Forests in the west. The quiet countryside, with its many unspoilt villages and historic towns, extends northwards to join the particularly beautiful Constable Country on the Suffolk border.

CHESHIRE

Pop., 933,200; RV, £138,511,000; Rate Precept, 169·0p; Debt, £149,000,000; Area, 232,842 hectares.

Length of Highways (kilometres) Motorway 113; Motorway sliproads 69·02; Trunk 206·01; Principal 685·59; Other 4,387·62; Unsurfaced 160; Footpaths 3,166·9.

Community Homes: 17; Community Home (with Education on Premises): 1; Community Homes Group One Assessment: 3; Homes for Mentally Handicapped Children: 4; Residential Nursery: 1; Elderly Persons Homes: 60; Intermediate Treatment: 1; Day Centres for the Elderly & Physically Handicapped: 31; Community Centre: 1; Hostel for Recovering Mentally Ill: 1; Home: 1; Homes for Mentally Handicapped Adults: 9; Home for Physically Handicapped Adults: 1; Day Centres for Children: 4; Day Nurseries: 11; Playgroups: 4; Day Centres for Elderly: 6; Adult Training Centres: 8; Day Centres for Physically Handicapped: 5; Sheltered Workshop: 1; Gypsy/Travellers Sites: 5; Schools—Nursery: 3 (plus 68 Nursery classes attached to primary schools); Primary: 482; Secondary: 77; Special: 26; Colleges of Further/Higher Education: 7; College of Agriculture: 1; Youth Clubs: 25; Teachers Centres: 3; Outdoor Education Centres: 7; Education Centres: 2; Museums: 3; Libraries: 55; Library Centres: 10; Mobiles and Trailers: 8; School Mobiles: 2; Police Stations: 28.

Parliamentary Constituencies (10): City of Chester; Congleton; Crewe and Nantwich; Eddisbury; Ellesmere Port and Neston; Halton; Macclesfield; Tatton; Warrington North; Warrington South.

EEC Constituencies (2): Cheshire East, Cheshire West.

Petty Sessional Divisions: 8.

Regional Water Authorities: (1) North-West; (2) Welsh.

Audit by District Auditor (No. 5 Audit District).

DISTRICT COUNCILS IN THE COUNTY

Chester (City), Congleton (B), Crewe and Nantwich (B), Ellesmere Port and Neston (B), Halton (B), Macclesfield (B), Vale Royal, Warrington (B).

TOPOGRAPHY

Prior to local government reorganisation, Cheshire's boundaries had remained substantially unchanged since Domesday.

In 1974, the shape, size and character of the county were all substantially changed. Large areas, largely urbanised, were surrendered to the new Merseyside County Council (in north Wirral), and to Greater Manchester County (around the southern fringe of the conurbation); Tintwistle in the north-east passed to Derbyshire. Cheshire received in return the two county boroughs of Chester and Warrington, together with Widnes, the rural district of Warrington and part of the Golborne Urban District—all, like Warrington County Borough, formerly in Lancashire.

The result is a more compact county with no part more than about an hour's journey by road (mostly by Cheshire's excellent motorway system). While marginally smaller in population, it is expected that new Cheshire will reach a million again during the 1980s.

Above all, new Cheshire is socially and economically well balanced. Now that the whole of the Mersey belt of heavily industrialized towns (including the New Towns of Runcorn and Warrington which continue to expand rapidly) between Merseyside and Manchester on both sides of the Manchester Ship Canal is within one county, there are great opportunities for environmental experiment and improvement to match the industrial investment and employment of the area. The brine deposits which have been so important to mid-Cheshire for centuries are a national asset, and their products are processed by the heavy chemical industry in the Mersey belt. Similarly the County deposits of building and silica sand are vital to the construction and foundry industries.

Agriculture (especially Dairy farming) remains important of course, and contributes to the variety of Cheshire's landscape which ranges from the gritstone of the Pennines east of Macclesfield (part of the Peak District National Park) to the rolling plains of North and South Cheshire with their striking sandstone escarpments at Alderley Edge, Helsby and Broxton. This natural beauty is enhanced by Cheshire's proximity to other National Parks in Snowdonia and the Lake District, and to the Welsh coastline.

Activity 8

Read the information provided by Cheshire and Essex County Councils, and the background details from the Municipal Yearbook regarding the two authorities.

Bearing in mind the information given above complete the following questions:

a What is the difference in rate poundage between the two authorities? Why do you think the variation exists?

b What are the major areas of expenditure for the two counties? Why do you think there are differences in the level of expenditure on various services?

c Both information leaflets use pie charts to indicate their sources of income. Compare the amounts obtained by the two counties from the different sources, and account for any differences you observe.

In order to make comparison easier, it may be helpful to convert the Essex figures into percentages.

d On the Cheshire leaflet two simple pie charts are included showing *The Financing of Net Expenditure 1975–76* and *1985–86*. What do these pie charts tell you about changes in the way in which expenditure is financed? Explain why these changes have taken place.

Summary of skills

The intention of the study involved in this unit is not only to learn facts about organizations but also to develop skills which will be of use in the business world. This section at the end of each block of work is to indicate the skills areas you should have developed during each activity.

Skills

Skill	*Activities in which skill is developed*
a Information gathering	All activities
b Learning and studying	All activities
c Communicating	1, 6, 8
d Design and visual discrimination	1
e Numeracy	2, 3, 4, 6, 7, 8
f Working with others	6, 8

Links with other units

You should also appreciate the links which exist between your studies in this area and your studies of *People in Organizations* and *Finance*. The activities are related to the understanding of organizational structures and the interpretation of information which you will examine as part of the *People in Organizations* unit. In the *Finance* unit you will develop your understanding of the sources of finance available to organizations within the public sector.

Block 4
Objectives and Policies

Introduction

As we have seen from the examination of the public and private sectors within the mixed economy, there are a variety of organizations involved in the provision of goods and services. Some of these organizations have very similar features, others differ very widely. The aim of this block of work is to examine the variety of objectives and policies which organizations may pursue, and to investigate the process of policy formulation by both private sector business organizations and public sector organizations.

Organizations

An organization is a group of individuals working together to achieve specific aims or goals over a period of time. If we compare a business organization and a voluntary organization we can see how both organizations fit that definition.

The Imperial Group PLC has a number of different divisions comprising the activities of the Group. They include:

1 Imperial Tobacco Ltd., incorporating W.D. & H.O. Wills, John Player & Sons, and Ogdens.

2 Imperial Brewing & Leisure Ltd., which includes the following well-known activities: Courage beer, John Smith's Bitter, Happy Eater family roadside restaurants, Welcome Break motorway service areas, newsagents, off-licences, etc.

3 Imperial Foods Ltd., which includes Ross Foods, Golden Wonder, HP foods, sauces and canned foods.

4 Howard Johnson Company: this is one of the United States' leading hotel and restaurant organizations.

The main aim of the group is to make a profit, as a quote from the Chairman's Statement (*Report and Accounts 1984*) indicates:

'Imperial as a whole made good progress in 1984. The three UK Divisions produced significantly higher operating profits and, helped by a lower interest charge and effective tax rate, the Group's pre-tax and after tax earnings increased by 13% and 16% respectively.'

Bird Protection Today
The work of the RSPB

WHO WE ARE AND WHAT WE DO

With all the publicity the Royal Society for the Protection of Birds receives for its work, most people have heard of us – even if some occasionally get us confused, through the similarity of initials, with the RSPCA (with whom we do in fact work closely in some of our activities).

WILD BIRDS
Our concern is with **wild** birds – in the words of our Royal Charter 'birds and their place in nature'. When you visit our reserves, do not expect us to show you birds confined in cages or aviaries. We want you to share the beauty and fascination of birds living free in their natural surroundings. You will find this requires a little patience and skilled observation (and a pair of binoculars helps enormously). 'Free as a bird' is no empty phrase when it comes to observing wildlife!

OUR MEMBERS
Our members – and there are over 360,000 of them – include people of all ages from all walks of life. A minority are expert ornithologists able to identify the rarest bird without hesitation, but most simply take pleasure in seeing the wild birds of garden, countryside and seashore, would like to know more about them, and care enough about their survival for the benefit of future generations to support an organisation geared to take effective action on their behalf.

And the RSPB really is effective, for it is today Europe's largest voluntary wildlife conservation body. With a highly professional staff, and the enthusiastic backing of its many members, it has the will and the means to oppose those whose activities threaten our birds and could rapidly cause the disappearance of many species from our shores.

The dangers to birds come from many quarters: from loss of habitat through modern economic farming and forestry practice: from the development of industry, communications and the extraction and transport of oil; from the widespread pursuit of countryside leisure; from the thoughtless and deliberate use of poisons; from illegal egg-collecting, trapping, shooting and the illicit trade in rare species of birds.

Extracts from a Royal Society for the Protection of Birds booklet.

The Royal Society for the Protection of Birds (RSPB) on the other hand has existed for some years with its major objective, 'to encourage the conservation of wild birds by developing public interest in their beauty and place in nature.'

Activity 1

Identify one example of each of the following,
a a sole trader
b a public limited company
c a central government department
d a voluntary organization.

Research the objectives and aims of each of the organizations which you have chosen. Identify as many as possible for each organization, not just the one which you consider to be the most important. Note to what extent the objectives of your organizations are similar and to what extent they differ.

When you have done that, against each objective listed for each of the organizations, try to suggest a suitable policy which the organization might pursue in order to achieve that objective.

When you have completed your list, or if you are having difficulty, read through the following section.

Objectives and policies

Any organization will set aims or objectives which it seeks to achieve. The success of an organization will be measured against the extent to which its aims are secured. There is therefore a direct relationship between the aims and objectives of an organization and its policy decisions.

Management by objectives (MBO)

The overall plans and objectives of an organization, broken down into more detailed objectives and budgets for each function and department within the organization provide the basis for management by objectives (MBO). The overall organizational aims and objectives provide the general objectives for senior managers within the organization who will meet regularly in order to discuss the progress in achieving the objectives set.

Senior managers then set relevant objectives within the general context of the organizational objectives in order to provide detailed objectives for their departmental managers and supervisors. Through this process detailed targets for each member of staff are formulated, and thus overall objectives of the organization should be achieved.

The MBO technique does however have its drawbacks because it tends to emphasize what is measurable, eg increasing sales, and tends to exclude those aspects of work which it is less easy to quantify. In addition there may be a tendency for staff to set objectives which are easily achievable so that overall performance is hardly affected.

Policy decisions

Policy decisions affect all aspects of an organization. They provide a frame-work for organizational activity, stating what people in organizations must or must not do.

In private business organizations, policy decisions will be made by management and the board of directors. In government organizations, policy will be laid down by statute (laws passed by parliament) and guidelines will also be issued by rules and regulations which are produced by ministers with the help of senior civil servants.

Objectives, policies and the private sector

The objectives which are set by organizations will clearly vary considerably, depending on the exact nature of the organization involved. However the prime objective for any commercial organization is the need to survive and, in order to do this, the need to make a profit and to maintain sales.

These primary objectives of achieving survival, profitability and sales can be achieved by pursuing a wide range of secondary objectives linked directly to the functions of the organizations, eg marketing, investment, production, etc.

The range of policy decisions made in order to achieve stated objectives will of necessity be very wide. For a business organization, policy must provide a framework for all organizational activity. The following examples illustrate the range of policy.

1 *Marketing policy*

The board of directors will normally make policy decisions on the mix of products which the company is to be involved in marketing. Many firms identify as an objective the need to increase their market share (ie the amount of the total market which they sell to). In recent years, for example, British-based car manufacturers have identified increased market share as a major objective as they have endeavoured to win back sales from foreign competition. There are a number of policies which organizations might adopt to increase their market share:

1 increasing advertising to final users of the product in an attempt to win customers from competitors,
2 increasing production in order to reduce unit cost and reduce selling price, thus being more competitive,
3 a merger with, or take-over of a company operating in the same market,
4 improving the quality or performance of the product, eg car manufacturers introducing new models.

2 *Investment policy*

Investment programmes provide new buildings, plant or equipment, and they may be undertaken in order to achieve a number of different objectives. For example the need to regain lost market share or to reverse falling sales may be achieved by alternative policies, depending upon the situation facing a company, for example:

1 carrying out a programme of research and development to produce new products which can take over from product lines which are beyond technical improvement,

2 carrying out research and development in the area of production techniques,

3 investing in the introduction of new technology and production processes in order to benefit from reduced costs,

4 expanding the business through the process of amalgamation.

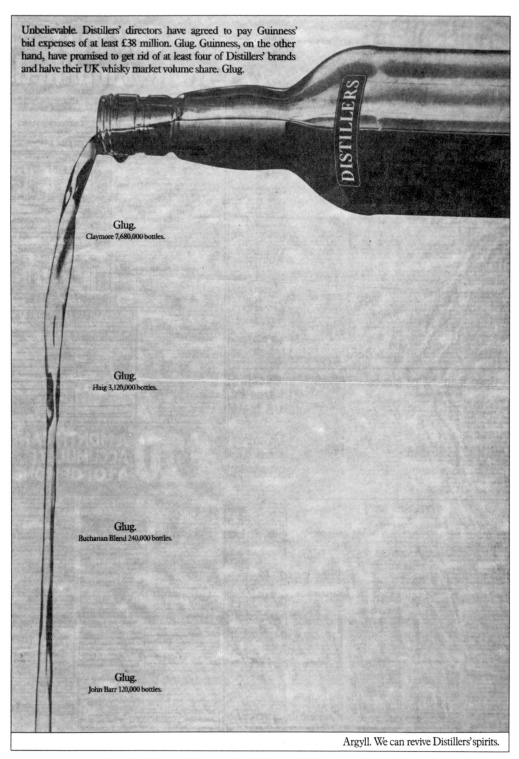

An advertisement to promote a take-over bid.

BIDS AND DEALS

Boots, the high street chemist and pharmaceutical producer, made an agreed £19 million bid for the 86 optician shops run by **Clement Clarke (Holdings).**

The Monopolies and Mergers Commission is to consider the £149 million hostile take-over bid launched by **London International Group,** the consumer products and contraceptives company, for **Wedgwood,** the fine china manufacturer.

Sealink British Ferries paid £5 million for **Hoverspeed,** the cross Channel hovercraft company.

Lonrho, the international trading company, provided £18 million of backing for the **Today** newspaper and acquired 35 per cent of the equity.

Beecham, the pharmaceuticals and chemicals company, is selling off fringe activities, including its home improvements products division.

Dixons, the electrical retailers, increased its take-over bid for **Woolworth Holdings** by £350 million to £1.82 billion.

Financial newspapers provide regular information about mergers and take-overs.

We have already seen that one way of reducing competition and gaining greater control over a particular market is for a firm to expand through the process of amalgamation. With a merger, the firms concerned agree to amalgamate. In a take-over one firm, without necessarily having the consent of the other firm, acquires sufficient shares to have a controlling interest.

Another motive for the acquisition of other companies is to provide greater security for the organization by extending its activities into another stage of its existing production, eg a brewery may expand vertically towards the market by securing more retail outlets in the form of public houses and off-licences. Organizations may also diversify by extending their product range and activities, eg the Rank Organization is involved in films, bread, hotels, dance halls and office copiers.

Growth by merger or amalgamation is usually referred to as **integration**. Three basic types of integration exist.

Horizontal integration This occurs when firms engaged in producing the same kind of good or service are brought under unified control. The Westminster Bank and the National Provincial Bank joining together to form the National Westminster Bank is a clear example of a horizontal

merger. One problem which may arise due to horizontal
integration, since there will clearly be a reduction in
competition, is monopoly.

Horizontal integration.

In many cases horizontal combination is carried out in
order to obtain economies of scale (which will provide a
reduction in costs). These falling costs due to the growth in
the size of the organization may arise for a variety of
reasons, eg,
1 average raw material costs can be reduced through
   discounts on bulk buying,
2 average production costs may fall because specialist
   personnel and technologically advanced plant can be used,
3 the cost of borrowing can be reduced as financial
   institutions tend to charge a lower rate of interest on larger
   loans,
4 the average cost of marketing and distributing products
   may fall.

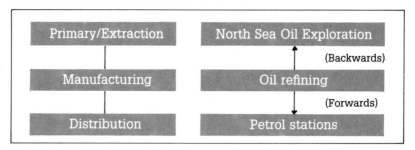

Vertical integration.

Vertical integration This occurs when two or more firms at
different stages of the production process combine, eg a
motor manufacturer may acquire a car components firm or a
brewery acquire public houses. When the movement is
towards the source of supply this may indicate a desire on the
part of the firm to exercise greater control over the quantity
and quality of its supplies. If the movement is towards the
market outlets then there is usually a desire to ensure that
outlets are available to the firm and to raise the standard of
service to the customer.

Conglomerate mergers These involve the take-over of one firm by another which largely produces a different product, eg Sears (Holdings) is involved in a wide range of activities including shipbuilding, footwear products and insurance.

Although the output of a large conglomerate may appear to be made up of a range of very different products, the diversification of output is not usually completely random. The products chosen are often linked by the use of common raw materials, common technology or common market outlets.

Whatever the reason for the expansion of activities the board of directors of the company concerned will be involved in making important investment decisions.

Activity 2	By examining the financial pages of the national daily newspapers or the business sections of the Sunday papers, identify organizations which are involved in a take-over or merger. Examine the motives and attitudes of the two companies involved.

3 Production policy

Policies concerning production may initially be concerned with the issues of the location of the production plant, the scale at which the plant might operate, and what type of production process will be adopted. Once these strategic issues have been settled, then objectives and policy pass to another level. Production policies will often have to respond to marketing information.

A robotic system performing combined assembly, inspection and measuring tasks during the manufacture of domestic televisions.

For example, if a company runs three product lines and research shows that one is selling badly and the other two well, then it will be necessary to alter the production mix.

If a firm establishes the objective of reducing production costs, then the policy pursed by the production department may be to replace labour with capital by introducing automated processes and new technology, eg the use of robots on car production lines.

4 Purchasing policy

One of the key inputs into any organization is that of materials and equipment. The purchasing department will be responsible for the acquisition and control of these items.

Probably the overriding objective of a purchasing department is to buy in materials and equipment of suitable quality at the lowest cost without jeopardizing continuity of production. Various policies are possible.

1 Buy as and when materials and equipment are required, ie buy only the quantities needed for current production requirements. The advantage is a saving in storage and administration costs, but the purchase of small quantities may be more costly without the possibility of quantity discounts.

2 Buy for a long-term period and carry stocks of materials and equipment. The advantages and disadvantages are virtually reversed. The firm will require storage space and these costs will be greater, but quantity discounts should be available and administrative and handling costs are reduced. In addition the risks of production being interrupted are reduced. If the materials and equipment are subject to price fluctuations, then firms will try to buy in quantity when prices are low, but of course there is no way of telling whether prices will fall yet further.

5 Manpower policy

Manpower policies deal with the selection and recruitment of employees, training and promotion, dismissal procedures, etc. The features of manpower planning are discussed in more detail in Block 1.

The main features of the policy will be the estimates of the numbers of employees which the organization will need and the type of experience and qualifications required.

Policy changes

The range of policies identified above is not intended to provide an exhaustive list of policy areas, but merely to provide some examples. Policy decisions affect the whole range of activities of an organization and provide a guide for further decision-making.

Policy formulation and planning is a permanent process in most organizations. During the establishment of a business, many policy decisions will be made, but as the organization grows and as circumstances change, further policies will be formulated.

One external factor which may require policy changes is a change in legislation. For example the Health and Safety at Work Act 1974 laid down the principles relating to health and safety, and clarified the duties of the employer and employees. One of the employer's duties under the Act is to produce a Safety Policy Statement and communicate that policy to all employees. A more recent piece of legislation, which will affect the policy of many organizations with regard to the holding of personal data, is the Data Protection Act 1984. The details below indicate how the recent legislation will affect organizations.

Personal data and the need for policy: a case study

Data Protection Act 1984

In outline the Act attempts to protect individuals against the misuse or abuse of information held about them when it is processed electronically. The Act gives individuals the right to be told what information about them as individuals is held on computer files. If the information is found to be wrong, then individuals have the right to have the records corrected. The Act also provides for the subject of personal data to obtain compensation from a data user for damage resulting from the loss or unauthorized disclosure of data, and inaccuracy of data.

Personal data

Personal data is information which relates directly to living individuals: name, address, date of birth, qualifications, etc.

Provisions of the Act

The Act established a *Data Protection Register*. Computer users are required to register all of their computer applications which handle personal data. The Registrar will maintain a public register of users, computer bureaux and applications.

Individuals will be able to find out from the Register what sort of personal data is held by an organization. The individual can then go along to a particular organization and ask to be given a copy of the personal data held on him/her. If the information is incorrect then the organization may be liable for civil damages, and if they do not correct the information then they will be in breach of the law.

Implications for all organizations

1 The need to assess the extent to which the Act will affect the various business operations. There are some exemptions, eg data held for crime detection, tax assessment or immigration control. For ordinary business organizations, some payroll and accounting data may be exempt from certain provisions.
2 Identification of systems which require registering.
3 The need to review data held to see if it needs revision, in terms of the purposes for which the data is held, the classes and subjects of the data, and its sources and disclosures.

Organizations are expected to follow certain principles in maintaining and processing personal data. These include taking measures to ensure that information is accurate, up to date, obtained fairly and lawfully, and protected from unauthorized access by appropriate security measures.

The Act will undoubtedly necessitate the identification of someone with responsibility within an organization for ensuring compliance with the Act.

In many organizations the job of Data Protection Officer may not be a full-time job in itself. However, even small organizations will need to identify the individual responsible for data protection. Who can take this responsibility will depend upon the organizational structure and the abilities of individuals: the Company Secretary, Personnel Manager or Administration Manager would be at an appropriate level.

In order to comply with the Data Protection Act and to take into account all its implications, many organizations have sought to produce their own policy for the protection of personal data. Such policy has been laid down in the form of a detailed code of practice or a broad set of principles. IBM has produced a set of principles (see below) backed up by examples and detailed guidelines.

IBM policy document for the protection of personal data.

IBM internal programme for the protection of personal data

Main principles and practices

1 Purpose definition The purpose(s) of any file or application that makes use of personal data should be clearly defined and shown to be in support of valid IBM business needs.

2 Collection and use limitation Only the personal data that is needed for the defined purpose(s) of an application or file may be collected. It should be collected by fair and lawful means and from reliable sources. It should be correct, complete and kept up-to-date, and be used and retained on the active file only to the extent necessary for the defined purpose(s) of the application on file.

3 Access and communication limitation Within one IBM company, personal data should be made available only to data users/recipients with a well defined need-to-know. Communication of personal data outside the IBM company that holds that data should be avoided insofar as possible. Such data should be anonymised or aggregated whenever feasible in order to avoid identification of the data subject.

To data users/recipients outside IBM, personal data should be communicated only:
when required for legal reasons, or
when required for valid business reasons when legally permitted, or
when requested by the data subject concerned.

Accountability and data security

The person responsible for an application or file that makes use of personal data must be identified. All information containing personal data must be carefully classified and protected against unauthorised or accidental disclosure, modification or destruction.

Data subject involvement

IBM honours justified requests from data subjects to have data related to them corrected, completed or updated. Insofar as compatible with its valid business interests and applicable legal requirements, IBM also honours data subjects' requests for information about data related to them that is collected, stored and used by IBM, about the sources of that data and about data users/recipients outside the company to whom such data is communicated.

Activity 3

Identify a local business organization and find out how it is complying with the needs of the Data Protection Act. You should be aware that, although the Act became law in July 1984, its full provisions will not be felt until mid-1987.

Objectives and policy in the public sector

We have already seen that public sector organizations can be broadly grouped under three main headings: public corporations, government departments and local authorities. These organizations, like any in the private sector, will attempt to set specific objectives and thus determine policies which will achieve those objectives.

Some of the public corporations, eg British Steel Corporation, operate very much on commercial objectives, seeking greater efficiency and profitability. This means operating on objectives and policies which are very similar to firms in the private sector. However, at certain times in the past, even those public corporations which are firmly based in the commercial sector have had their objectives and policies determined by wider economic and social criteria rather than commercial criteria. For example, in the past, funds were used by British Coal to keep open pits in areas of high unemployment because of the adverse social effects which closure would entail. Acting purely on commercial criteria, British Coal might have chosen to close pits.

British Rail is a public corporation which has to consider both commercial and social objectives: below are examples of possible objectives and policies which it might pursue.

Objectives	**Policies**
To provide transport facilities in rural areas where alternative means of transport are limited.	Maintenance of loss-making routes in rural areas; indentification of the need for a social subsidy.
To increase efficiency in the operation of the rail service.	Introduction of one-man operated trains. Introduction of flexible rostering for personnel.
To increase usage of trains at off-peak times and so increase revenue.	Introduction of cheap fares at off-peak times.

Central Government departments of course will to a great extent have their objectives and policies determined by the political decisions of the government of the day, and by legislation in existence. Let us look at some of the possible objectives and resulting policies of the Department of Education and Science.

Objectives	Policies
That all citizens should receive a standard of education which enables them to participate fully in economic and social life.	Provision of a state education system for all children from 5–16.
Increase in literacy and numeracy amongst those who failed to acquire these skills during normal schooling.	Establishment of a numeracy and literacy programme across the country, with the allocation of specific funds.
To prepare those of school age for the technology available in work situations.	Provision of specific funds for the purchase of computer hardware and software in schools.
To encourage a larger number of people to continue their full-time education beyond the age of 16.	Provision of grants for all students over the age of 16.

Activity 4

The Employment and Training Act 1973 established the Manpower Services Commission (MSC) which is responsible for industrial training.
a How is the MSC linked to central government?
b What are the MSC's objectives?
c Identify MSC policies and explain who determines the policy.

Local authority departments will also formulate objectives and policies in response to the political make-up of the local council. Again, if we examine one particular department, then it is possible to identify some possible objectives and policies. Below are some possibilities for a local authority Planning Department.

Objectives	Policies
To interpret national and regional policies, particularly those relating to the economic planning and development of the region.	The encouragement of new firms and expansion of existing firms in the area through the provision of advanced factories, roads, sewers and other services.

To improve the physical environment of an area and to conserve its natural resources.

The requirement of a phased and orderly extraction of minerals within an area whilst maintaining control over the amount of dereliction, dust, noise and traffic generated.

To maintain existing housing within a particular area, rather than clearing and redeveloping.

Designation of areas as Housing Action Areas or General Improvement Areas with provision of grants to pay for renovation.

Activity 5

Working in groups, choose one area of activity with which your local authority is concerned, eg conservation within the planning process or provision of housing within the authority (you may need some help from your tutor to select a suitable area for study).

a Investigate the objectives and policies identified by the local authority in your chosen area.

b Identify the decision-making process within the authority which produces local authority policy.

Activity 6

Part-time students

Examine your employing organization with a view to identifying its objectives, and the policies which it has pursued to achieve them.

If you work in a commercial organization, then it may help to identify the overall objectives and then to look at the specific objectives and policies which are linked directly to the functions of the organizations, eg Marketing, Production, Investment, etc.

If you work within the public sector in an area which is not directly involved in commercial activity, eg a local authority housing department, then it may be suitable for you to identify the overall objectives of the authority but then to examine the specific objectives of your particular department and the policies linked to those objectives.

Full-time students

Choose a large commercial organization and investigate its objectives and the policies which it has established in order to achieve them. It will be useful to identify, not only the primary objectives, but also the secondary objectives which are linked to the functions of Marketing, Investment, Production, etc. Whichever type of organization you examine, you are required to:

a Identify the objectives of the organization and the policies introduced to achieve them.
b Comment on the effect of these policies on individuals and organizations not directly connected with the organization, eg competitors, suppliers, customers, local communities, government departments, etc.
c Constructively criticize the policies identified and evaluate their ability to achieve stated objectives.
d Your findings should be organized for submission as a formal report. In addition, you are required to give a ten-minute presentation of your findings to the rest of your group.

Conclusion

In this block we have examined a wide range of objectives and policies within the public and private sectors. We have seen clearly the direct relationship which exists between the aims and objectives of an organization and its policy decisions. Policy decisions once made have to be implemented, and it is policy which provides a framework for the activities of the various departments within an organization. Departments will need to provide information on their performance in order to establish the success of the policy in meeting its stated objectives.

Summary of skills

The intention of the study involved in this unit is not only to learn facts about organizations, but also to develop skills which will be of use in the business world. This section at the end of each block of work is to indicate the skills areas you should have developed during each activity.

Skills

Skill	*Activities in which skill is developed*
a Information gathering	All activities
b Learning and studying	All activities
c Communicating	1, 3, 4
d Working with others	1, 2, 4
e Information processing	3

Links with other units

You should also appreciate the links which exist between your studies in this area and your studies of *People in Organizations* and *Finance*. These activities are related to organizational structures and operations, and electronic technology which you will examine as part of the *People in Organizations* unit. In the *Finance* unit you will use financial information to measure performance against objectives of organizations.

Block 5
Organizations and Decisions

Introduction

This block examines the identification of problems within an organization and the decision-making processes and the organizational structures involved. We start off by looking at some problems within a further education college and then look at a business organization which is changing location.

All organizations need to make decisions in order to operate smoothly. Experience suggests that although no two decisions are the same, there are common features in most decisions. Isolating and understanding these factors should help us to understand decision-making processes more clearly. In this block we will examine the processes involved in decision-making in two different organizations.

Broadfield Further Education College

Broadfield College is the Further Education college which serves a large town of about 120 000 people. The college's work is divided into five departments, Food and Fashion, Humanities and Business Studies, Secretarial Studies, Art and Design, and Engineering. The college has 600 full-time students and many more part-time students attending on a block, day-release and evening basis.

At a recent meeting of the Common Services Committee, various complaints and problems were raised about students' use of common facilities. The Common Services Committee discusses the provision of all the facilities of the college which are available to staff and students, eg heating, refectory facilities, etc. It makes recommendations for improvements when necessary and suggests changes in operation where needed. The committee reports to the Academic Board which is the major committee in the organizational structure of the college, comprising the Principal, departmental heads, local authority representatives, representatives of teaching staff, and representatives of students.

The discussion was initiated by a representative from the Secretarial Department, who complained that students were consuming food and drink in teaching rooms. They were leaving wrappers and cartons all over the floor and in particular this was happening in rooms which housed expensive machinery, eg word processors and microcomputers.

A student representative broke into the discussion saying that it was hardly surprising that students ate their lunch in classrooms as they had nowhere else to go. The previous year the student common room had been taken over and converted into a computer workshop because of a shortage of suitable rooms.

The Chief Librarian also suggested that the library was experiencing problems with students using it as somewhere to sit, relax and talk, rather than for working. Library staff were concerned that much of their time was taken up asking students to be quiet rather than providing the information services which they were there for.

At this point the Vice-principal broke in and said that both she and the Principal were concerned that students congregated in the main entrance hall, first thing in the morning and at break and lunch times. Some students sat in the entrance hall and ate food. She expressed her concern over the impression that visitors would get as they entered the college.

The head of the college refectory also complained that students were bringing their own food in to eat and staying all lunchtime so that people buying meals in the refectory could not find places to sit.

The student representative suggested that many of these complaints arose from the loss of the common room and what was needed was a new building which could include a common room. The refectory opening hours did little to help the situation; 10.00 a.m. to 11.15 a.m.,

12.15 p.m. to 1.45 p.m., 3.00 p.m. to 4.00 p.m. In addition, the college hall was under–utilized. However, the Chief Administrative Officer did intervene to explain that the hall was well used in the summer term when examinations were held there nearly every day.

| *Activity 1* | Using information from the situation given above and from your own college organization, draw up an organization chart for Broadfield College. The organization chart should show the internal structure and should detail job titles and show the formal authority structure, ie who reports to whom. The following people/committees need to appear on your chart: the Chief Librarian, Vice-principal, Heads of all five departments, teaching staff, Principal, Chief Administrative Officer, the Academic Board, library staff.

Complete this task before continuing.

Organization charts

An organization chart is a way of showing the internal structure of any organization. It is a visual aid, which should detail the various job titles and indicate the formal authority structure. In drawing up an organization chart you should note the following points:
1 The chart is composed of a number of boxes joined together.
2 Decide whether to use a vertical or horizontal chart. (The chart showing the structure of a college of further education is a vertical chart.)
3 Try to portray the structure as it actually operates.
4 Job titles should appear in the boxes.
5 The chart should have a clear title.
6 Keep the chart simple and ensure the boxes are well spaced.

You can check your organization chart for Broadfield College with that given on the next page. This is an organization chart for another college but shows a very similar structure to the one which you should have identified.

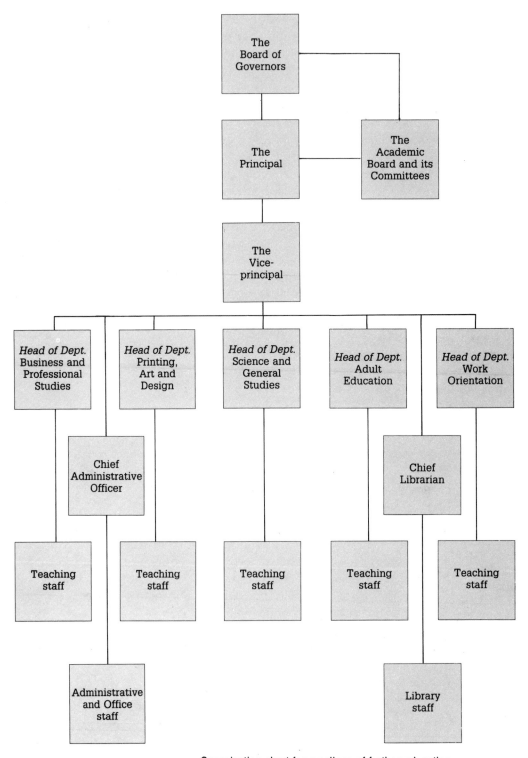

Organization chart for a college of further education.

Activity 2	Using the case of Broadfield College and the information included, answer the following questions.

1 What problems can you identify in relation to the facilities available to students within the college?
2 Why has the problem over facilities arisen?
3 Suggest some of the conflicts which might arise due to the problems identified.
4 Design a short questionnaire which would enable you to find out what facilities students wanted.
5 Suggest the alternatives which would be available to college management in order to overcome the problems identified.
6 Recommend a best solution and suggest the process which would have to be gone through in order to implement it. Identify the people and structures involved. An examination of the authority structure in your own college may help you to do this.

Now you have completed your analysis of Broadfield College, you can check your findings by examining the theory of decision-making in more detail.

Stages in the decision-making process

1 Defining the problem

It may appear that problems should be quite clear and obvious. That is not, however, always the case. The issue that first comes to the manager's attention may only be a manifestation of a much bigger problem. In the case of Broadfield College the initial problem was that students were eating their lunch in classrooms: a decision may therefore have been taken simply to lock the rooms in order to exclude the students. This would not however solve the problem as further discussion showed. Those students excluded from the classrooms would merely have added to the problems in the refectory, library and main entrance hall. The root of these problems was that the students had no common-room facilities.

Identification of problems within an organization should also take into account the objectives of the organization, to ensure that possible solutions will not conflict with the overall aims of the organization.

In diagnosing a problem it is also important to recognize the constraints which exist and which will limit the action open to management.

In the case of Broadfield College the problem over student use of facilities appears to have arisen due to the withdrawal of the common-room facilities. The college was constrained by the number of rooms available and decided to use the student common room for computing facilities. At the time that decision was made, account should have been taken of the effect on student facilities. It would appear that what the college really needs is more rooms, but this brings us to another constraint. The college will have to adapt to changes in the level of economic activity. It would seem likely that given recent restrictions on local authority spending the local council will not have been able or willing to allocate funds for the building of an extension.

2 *Information and analysis*

Organizations generate a great deal of information in formulating and reviewing plans. When a problem arises much of the information required for the solution may already be available. There may, however, be a need to collect further information, to aid in the solution of the problem.

A commercial organization may at this point be faced with the problem of whether or not it should collect more information and at what cost. It can be the case that the time and money involved in obtaining more information outweighs the improvement expected in the quality of the decision. Firms may therefore take a decision and make adjustments later if and when more information becomes available.

In Broadfield College's case, you were asked to design a short questionnaire in order to provide further information on student needs.

3 *Examining the alternatives*

In the course of making decisions people are rarely presented with information which leads to one possible decision. In fact there are always two choices: to do something or leave things as they are and do nothing.

Analysis of the problem concerned and consideration of the constraints and the information available may well produce a number of alternative courses of action. There may also be some ideas which provide short-term solutions and can be put into operation quickly and others which are long-term solutions.

Some of the solutions which you may have considered in the case above include:
—opening the refectory for longer hours, setting aside an area for use by people bringing their own food,
—use of the hall in the autumn and summer term as a student common room,
—setting aside of a nonspecialist teaching room in each department for use by students over the lunch hour,
—in the long-term, acquiring funds from the local authority for a building programme to relieve the pressure on rooms.

4 *Implementation*

Once the choice has been made as to which alternative course of action is best, then it is necessary to execute or implement the decision. To complete the decision-making process the following points must be considered:
1 Decide who needs to take action and when.
2 Decide a timetable for implementation.
3 Determine how the decision is to be communicated to those affected.
4 Take action to counteract any adverse effects which the decision may have.
5 Ensure that the situation is reviewed at some time in the future.

In the work you completed for Activity 2, you were asked to examine the process of implementation. The exact nature of the process which you have identified will depend upon the solution which you chose.

If you had chosen the option of setting aside a non-specialist teaching room in each department for students to use over lunchtime, then the implementation process may have involved the following:
1 The Vice-principal meets with heads of department to ask them to designate one room within their department for use by students in the lunch hour.

2 Heads of Department confer with lecturing staff to determine the best room.

3 Memos are sent to all lecturing staff to inform them of the designated rooms and date of commencement; Course Tutors are asked to inform students of the facility.

4 Notices are placed on student noticeboards, and in the student newspaper, informing students of the rooms and their availability, and date of commencement.

5 Discussions take place with the caretaking and cleaning staff with regard to the designated rooms in case of extra cleaning requirements.

6 The decision is communicated to the Principal, Library and Refectory. Library staff and refectory staff are asked to provide feedback on the effect of the changes on their situation.

By analysing the problem faced by Broadfield College, you should now have a good idea of the process of decision-making.

Activity 3	Using the information from this block, draw up a flow diagram to show the stages identified in the decision-making process, starting with the identification of a problem and going through to the implementation of the decision. You can check your chart when completed with that given on page 109.

Having examined decision-making within a college you now have the opportunity to apply your understanding of the decision-making process to a specific business situation.

Fisher Engineering Ltd.

Fisher Engineering is a small engineering firm located in the town of Murcaster in the West Midlands. The firm produces specialist components for car manufacturers. Although it has faced difficulties in the past, with the help of new technology and the better fortunes of the car producers in the area, it now has full order books. Recently the Sales Department has negotiated a major new contract with one of the manufacturers in the area. Management considers that the upward trend in sales will continue and that in order to be able to cope with the level of orders the firm will need to move to larger premises.

The firm employs 250 people and is organized on a departmental basis, as shown below:

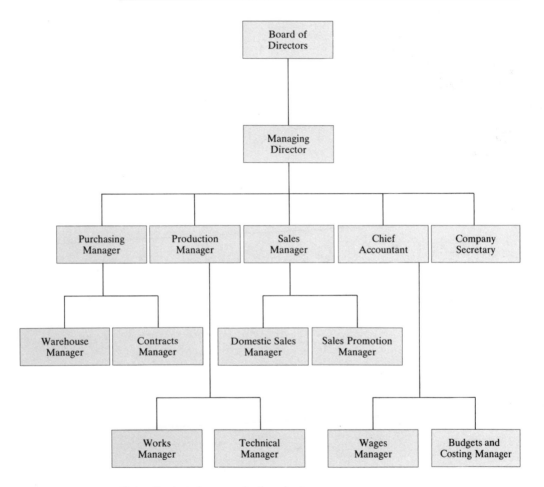

Fisher Engineering organization chart.

The present premises are close to the town centre in a Victorian area surrounded by improved houses where many of the employees live. The area has had the benefit of Council support for improvements and the firm itself took advantage of the grants available. The present site is therefore well maintained and there is local council interest in promoting its use as small workshops if Fisher Engineering decide to sell.

Renovated nineteenth century industrial premises.   A 'greenfields' industrial site.

Two realistic possibilities have been identified as new locations for the firm.

The first is a mid–Victorian warehouse about two miles from the present premises. The site was formerly a British Rail parcels depot. The building has been empty for a number of years. It stands in a substantial site with room for expansion but is in need of extensive repairs. The cost of the repairs would be offset by a relatively low purchase price. There would be ample parking space on and around the site.

The alternative is a factory on the Mellish Industrial Estate which is seven miles to the east of the town, equidistant from Murcaster and its neighbour Tadfield. The estate comprises a number of large units, although close by is a trading estate which caters for smaller firms. The vacant factory at this site is an ideal building, since it is a modern factory with good office space and plenty of parking all on one level. The site is to let and would allow the sort of production levels the firm is looking for, leaving room for some expansion in the future.

Activity 4 Using the stages in the decision-making process, indicate what you think are the important issues in arriving at a decision. Indicate what additional information (if any) you think might be necessary to reach a decision.

By considering each of the stages in the decision-making flow diagram you should be able to identify the important issues and the information required to reach a decision.

For example the first stage is concerned with problem diagnosis and the consideration of objectives and constraints. Your answer to Activity 4 would therefore include some or all of the following points:

Objectives of firm	—	to maintain profitability to increase production and meet sales targets
Constraints	—	present production capacity cost of moving and purchasing new site attitude of employees
Problem	—	the need to expand production at another site due to inadequate capacity at the present site

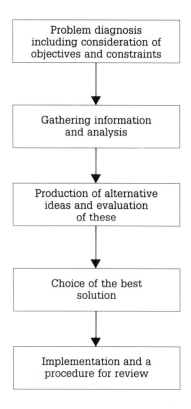

Flow diagram for the decision-making process.

Conclusion

On the completion of this block you should be aware of the formal organization structure which will exist in most organizations, and that the authority structure will affect the way in which decisions are made. In addition you should understand that it is possible to isolate common features within decisions which help us to have a clearer view of the decision-making process.

Summary of skills

The intention of the study involved in this unit is not only to learn facts about organizations, but also to develop skills which will be of use in the business world. This section at the end of each block of work is to indicate the skills areas you should have developed during each activity.

Skills

Skill	Activities in which skill is developed
a Design and visual discrimination	1, 3
b Learning and studying	All activities
c Communicating	1, 2, 3
d Information gathering	2, 4
e Identifying and tackling problems	2, 4

Links with other units

You should also appreciate the links which exist between your studies in this area and your studies of *People in Organizations* and *Finance*. These activities are related to organizational structures and presentation of information which you will examine as part of the *People in Organizations* unit. In the *Finance* unit you will examine the need for financial information to aid decision making.

Block 6
Organizations and Employment Legislation; Changing Life at Work

Introduction

This block is designed to help you to understand the present legal position of individuals in employment, and the changes which have taken place in this area.

In order to do this you will need to find out something about the working conditions first experienced by people who were in employment many years ago. Talking to parents or grandparents, or people of their age, would be suitable. You will then be able to compare your findings with the present situation.

Changes in employment legislation

We have already examined some of the legal rights of a new employee in Block 1, but now need to look more fully at employment law.

Firstly we need to identify the areas where legislation has been introduced to protect the individual employee. This should enable you to decide which questions you need to ask when carrying out your research into changing employment rights.

There will always be situations arising which may produce conflict between an organization and the individual employee. For example, what happens if

1 an employee arrives late for work on a number of occasions? Can the employer sack the employee?
2 an employer consistently fails to promote black workers because he thinks that the firm's customers would not like it?

3 an employer refuses to promote a woman worker because she may have children at some time in the future and the employer is worried about the demands which they might make on her time?

4 a woman worker becomes pregnant? Must she leave her job?

5 both a male and female worker with the same experience are doing the same job but one is paid more than the other? Should they receive the same wages?

6 a trade union branch secretary is refused time off to meet the full-time trade union official who is attending the workplace to discuss a member's grievance against management?

7 an employee is off sick from work for a long period? Is he/she still paid by the employer?

8 a business closes down and all the employees lose their jobs? Are they entitled to any compensation?

| *Activity 1* | Read through the eight situations given above. From your present knowledge suggest briefly what should happen in each case. |

Employment legislation

Each of the situations above concerns a particular area of legislation affecting the employee.

1 Protection against dismissal

2 Race discrimination

3 Sex discrimination

4 Maternity rights

5 Equal pay

6 Trade union activities/duties

7 Sick pay

8 Redundancy

It is these eight areas which we will be concerned with in this block of work. When you have completed this block you should be able to look back at these eight situations and compare your original ideas with your findings, after a careful examination of the changing rights of employees at work.

Activity 2	

Carry out an investigation of employment rights as they existed some time ago. In order to do this you will need to choose an individual who is willing to be interviewed to recount their recollection of working life when they were first at work. Parents or grandparents or some other person of their age would be ideal. You may wish to use a cassette recorder to record the interview, or alternatively you can note down the answers which your respondent gives. You will need to carry out the following procedure:

1 Write down the questions which you intend to ask of your respondent. You must give the questions careful consideration to ensure that you obtain the information you require on the eight areas identified above.

2 Identify your respondent and arrange an interview time.

3 Carry out the interview ensuring that you have an accurate record of the responses. If you do choose to use a cassette recorder, you will need to play the tape back and make some notes in order to have the responses readily to hand.

When you have completed your investigations, you will probably find that the responses vary according to the age of your respondent.

Below are some of the answers given by a respondent who was sixty-five years old and was talking about the employment rights which she experienced in 1935.

Question	**Response**
1 How easy was it for an employer to sack an employee?	Very easy, they just gave you notice when they no longer needed you.
2 Did women get the same pay as men for the same work?	No. Usually women were paid much less, even those doing the same work.
3 What happened if a woman became pregnant? Did she have to leave her job?	Yes. You might be able to work again later, but you had no right to return to your job.

These are just a few examples of responses to questions about working life fifty years ago. With the information which you have gathered from your own research, you should have a good idea of the employment rights which prevailed at the time that your respondent began work.

We need now to examine how the law protects individuals today and to what extent the situation has changed over the years.

Dismissal from work

1971 was the first time that employees were given the legal right not to be unfairly dismissed from their job. Prior to this, organizations had been able to hire and fire people as and when they needed to. This situation of course meant that individual employees had limited security in their jobs. In the late 1960s the trade union movement received considerable attention from both academics and politicians, culminating in a government report (the Donovan report) on trade unions and industrial relations. The Donovan report proposed that dismissal of an employee was justified only if there was a valid reason for it in connection with the capacity or conduct of the worker, or based on the operational requirements of the organization. Absence of such valid reasons would make dismissal unfair.

Under The Employment Protection (Consolidation) Act 1978, the law now states that employees have a right not to be unfairly dismissed and that those who think that they have been may seek a remedy by taking their complaint to an industrial tribunal.

Dismissal: information and procedures

Employees are treated as dismissed if:
—their contract of employment is terminated with or without notice,
—a fixed-term contract expires without being renewed,
—they leave their employment due to their employer's conduct, such that they are justified in terminating their employment without notice (constructive dismissal).

At this point an employee can only claim unfair dismissal if:
—they have worked for their employer for one year or more (two years if the employer has less than twenty workers),

—they are a full-time employee (part-timers working more than 16 hours per week and those working more than 8 hours per week with 5 years' continuous service count as full-time).

If the employee is entitled to make a claim for unfair dismissal, it must be lodged with an Industrial Tribunal within three months.

The employer must then prove that the employee was dismissed for one of the potentially fair reasons laid down in law. These reasons are set out below.

1 Capability or qualifications for the work which the employee must do: this covers employee incompetence, short and long-term sickness, and lack of qualifications to do the job.
2 Conduct: a wide range of misconduct has been said to justify dismissal. If an offence entails gross misconduct, then dismissal can take place without notice.
3 Redundancy: here the law is concerned with whether the employer acted reasonably in selecting employees for redundancy.
4 Situations where continued employment of a worker would be illegal, eg a driver who is disqualified from driving.
5 Some other substantial reason; this covers justifiable reasons which do not come under the above categories.

An employee claiming unfair dismissal may seek a remedy from an Industrial Tribunal. The Tribunals are independent judicial bodies which deal with complaints concerned with employment that are covered by the legislation. Each consists of a legally qualified chairman and two lay members, one appointed by an employer's panel and one appointed through the Trades Union Congress (TUC).

In determining claims of unfair dismissal the tribunal will use as a guide to fairness the code of practice Disciplinary Practices and Procedures in Employment issued by the Advisory, Conciliation and Arbitration Service (ACAS). The Code of Practice suggests that:

1 individuals should be informed of the complaints against them,
2 the employee should be given the opportunity to state his or her case,

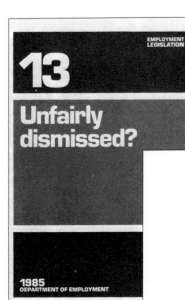

EMPLOYMENT
LEGISLATION

13

Unfairly
dismissed?

1985
DEPARTMENT OF EMPLOYMENT

Department of
Employment
guidelines.

Unfairly dismissed?

The Employment Protection (Consolidation) Act 1978 as amended by the Employment Act 1980 and the Employment Act 1982 gives most employees the right not to be unfairly dismissed.

This booklet outlines the unfair dismissal provisions of the Act and explains how complaints are dealt with. It gives general guidance only and should not be regarded as a complete or authoritative statement of the law.

Contents

3 individuals should have the right to be accompanied by a trade union representative or by a fellow employee when interviewed by management,
4 for minor offences, an employee should be given a formal oral warning or a written warning, making it clear that the warning is the first formal stage of the procedure,
5 further misconduct warrants a final written warning, prior to suspension or dismissal; a written statement of the reasons for dismissal should also be given.

Failure to adhere to this code is likely to make it difficult for the employer to argue that he acted fairly.

Employees who successfully bring a claim of unfair dismissal against their employers are entitled to:
1 Reinstatement: the employer must treat the employee as if the employment had not been terminated. Tribunals rarely order reinstatement because they take into account the employee's wishes and the practicalities involved.
2 Re-engagement: in this case the employee must be re-employed, but not necessarily in the same job.
3 Compensation: this is awarded if an employer is not ordered to re-employ the dismissed employee or if such an order is ignored. The basic award is the equivalent of a redundancy payment award. A compensatory award is based on an assessment of the employee's loss arising out of dismissal, eg loss of earnings, loss of expected wage increases and increments, loss of pension rights, the expense of looking for a new job.

If an employer has failed to comply with an order to re-employ an employee, then an additional award may be given. Such awards may be reduced if the tribunal believes that the employee's conduct contributed to their dismissal.

Discrimination by sex and race

The legislation covering these areas is dealt with by the Sex Discrimination Act 1975 and the Race Relations Act 1976.

Both Acts make it unlawful for an employer to discriminate on the grounds of sex, or against married persons, or on grounds of race, colour, nationality or ethnic or national origins. Discrimination by employers in recruitment and selection is covered, as well as in relation to existing employees.

Discrimination means treating someone less favourably, on the grounds of their race or sex, than anyone else would be treated under similar circumstances.

As far as sex discrimination is concerned, there is no discrimination if the presence of one sex is a genuine qualification, eg where the need for a particular sex is desirable in institutions where care or supervision is required, eg mental institutions and prisons. It is unfavourable treatment, however, if an employer discriminates against a woman in terms of employment opportunities and also opportunities for advancement, including promotion, training and transfer.

If sex discrimination is suspected, then a complaint can be made within three months of the discriminatory act to an industrial tribunal. The tribunal can make a statement regarding the complainant's rights, award compensation and recommend that the employer takes steps to remove discrimination in the future.

In addition to the right to take individual action, the Equal Opportunities Commission exists to identify and eliminate obstacles to equal opportunities. The Commission can conduct formal investigations either on its own initiative or at the request of the Secretary of State for Employment. It can issue a non–discriminatory notice against any employer; if such a notice is ignored an injunction can be taken out to enforce the relevant measures. An injunction is a court order prohibiting or requiring specific action.

The enforcement of the Race Relations Act 1976 is in the hands of the Commission for Racial Equality. It handles the complaints of aggrieved parties and also has the power to carry out its own formal investigations into cases of suspected discrimination. It too can issue a non–discrimination notice requiring changes in practices. An injunction can be obtained if necessary to enforce the notice.

Equal pay

The Equal Pay Act 1970 attempts to eliminate irregularities in pay between men and women doing broadly similar work. Prior to the Act there were many examples of substantial differences in pay between men and women performing the same task at the same speed.

EQUAL PAY

A guide to the Equal Pay Act

The Government is fully committed to the principle of equal pay for men and women in accordance with the UK's obligations under the European Equal Pay Directive. The Equal Pay Act is the means through which this principle is brought into effect, providing for individual women and men to apply to industrial tribunals for a just hearing of their claims.

This booklet gives general guidance to employees and employers about their rights and obligations under the Equal Pay Act 1970, as amended and supplemented by the Sex Discrimination Act 1975, the Employment Protection Act 1975 and The Equal Pay (Amendment) Regulations 1983.

Definitive interpretations of the provisions of the Act can be given only by the courts of law and by the industrial tribunals, to which disputes arising under the Act involving individuals may be referred, and by the Central Arbitration Committee.

Contents

Assuming a female worker wished to make a claim for equal pay, then it would be necessary to follow the procedure given below, by lodging a complaint with an Industrial Tribunal.

1 The applicant must select a male worker with whom she wishes to compare herself in order to make a claim. He must normally work at the same place and be employed under the same terms and conditions of employment.

2 The employee must be able to show

 i that she is employed on 'like work' to that of a man. 'Like work' is defined by the Act as being of 'the same or broadly similar nature' to the man's work.

or *ii* that she is in a job which, though different from that of a man, has been rated as equivalent under a job evaluation scheme.

or *iii* that she is employeed on work of equal value to a man's in terms of the skill, effort and decision-making involved.

Employment rights for the expectant mother

EMPLOYMENT LEGISLATION

4

Employment rights for the expectant mother

The maternity provisions set out in the Employment Protection (Consolidation) Act 1978, including the unfair dismissal provisions relating to maternity, have been amended by the Employment Act 1980 and the Employment Act 1982.

Contents

Maternity rights

Female employees have a number of legal rights during pregnancy and early motherhood.

Reasonable time off is available to pregnant women for antenatal care. A woman who has two years' continuous service by the eleventh week before her baby is due has the right to return to work after the birth. In order to exercise the right to maternity leave, a female employee must comply with the following procedure:

1 The employee must give 21 days' notice in writing of her intention to resign due to pregnancy, and state her intention to return to work, giving the date when the baby is expected.

2 49 days after the baby is due, the employer should write to the female employee, who must write back within 14 days confirming her intention to return to work.

3 The employee must give the employer at least 21 days' notice of her intention to return to work.

A female employee normally returns to work 29 weeks after the baby's birth. There is nothing to stop her from changing her mind and deciding that she will not return to work once the baby has been born.

On return a female employee should be allowed to return to her previous job unless it is not 'reasonably practicable'. If such a situation arises then she must be offered suitable alternative work.

If a woman qualifies for maternity leave then she will also be eligible for maternity pay. Maternity pay is normally nine-tenths of the weekly wage, and the employer makes the payment but can reclaim it in full from the state maternity fund.

The economically active of working age, plus a small number over retirement age, form the total labour force. The civilian labour force is the total labour force excluding those in HM Forces, and in mid-1984 is estimated to have numbered 26.4 million in Great Britain .... It increased by $1\frac{1}{2}$ million between 1971 and 1984, entirely because of the increase in the number of women in the civilian labour force over the period; the total is projected to increase by almost a further million by 1991. Overall, the proportion of women in the civilian labour force increased from 37 per cent in 1971 to 41 per cent in 1984; it is projected to be 42 per cent in 1991.

			Millions
	Males	Females	Total
Estimates			
1971	15.6	9.3	24.9
1976	15.6	10.1	25.7
1979	15.6	10.4	26.0
1981	15.6	10.6	26.2
1983	15.3	10.6	25.9
1984	15.5	10.9	26.4
Projections			
1986	15.6	11.2	26.8
1991	15.8	11.5	27.2

The civilian labour force: estimates and projections. (Source: Social Trends 1985)

Trade union activities/duties

Where a trade union is recognized by the employer for collective bargaining purposes, then members have the right to take unpaid time off for trade union activities, eg attending union meetings and conferences.

The representatives of the trade union have the right to paid time off for duties connected with industrial relations in the organization in which they work. These duties may include negotiations with management, communicating the results of negotiations to members, dealing with individual members' grievances and disciplinary cases, and consulting full-time officials of the union.

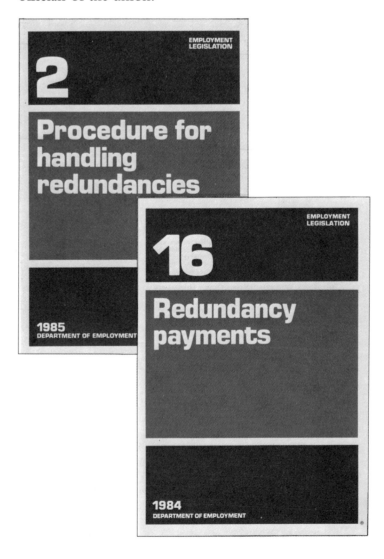

Redundancy

The term redundancy is used to refer to a situation where a business ceases to operate, or changes its location, or where the employer requires a smaller workforce for the existing work.

Over recent years redundancy for any of the three reasons above has been very common. Many firms have reduced their workforce, either because demand for their product has fallen, or because technology has replaced labour in the drive for greater efficiency.

Where an employee is made redundant, if they have two years' service or more then they are able to make a claim of redundancy against the employer and claim compensation. Scales of minimum compensation are laid down by law. The amount of the payment depends on the age of the employee and their length of service and pay.

In a unionized workplace the employer should consult the recognized trade union, and this may involve the negotiation of a procedure for handling redundancies. Legally the employer must consult the recognized trade union about every proposed redundancy. The law requires that unions have certain details, for example,

1 reasons for the proposed redundancies,
2 the numbers and details of the jobs and employees involved,
3 the proposed method of selecting employees for redundancy, eg requesting volunteers, last in first out,
4 the method of carrying out the redundancies, methods of payments, timing, etc.

This consultation with trade unions must take place as soon as possible and indeed, where large numbers are involved, there is a timetable laid down.

Some organizations which have needed to reduce the size of their labour force have encouraged workers nearing retirement age to retire early. Alternatively they have offered to pay those workers who volunteer for redundancy more than the statutory minimum.

Now that you have looked in detail at individual employees' rights in law, it should be possible for you to look back at the eight employment questions posed at the beginning of the block and formulate fuller answers than previously.

Refer to the eight questions on pages 111–12. Jot down some detailed answers to them in the light of your knowledge of employment law.

Now compare your answers with those which you first gave.

The context of changes in employment law

Over the last twenty-five years a substantial amount of legislation has been introduced by both Conservative and Labour governments to regulate the area of employment. In this block we have been concerned with legislation which has conferred rights on individual employees. The reasons for the changes in the law are complex, but it will be useful to examine briefly the historical, political and social context in which some of these changes took place.

Activity 4 Working in small groups of three of four, take one of the following areas:

> sex discrimination,
> racial discrimination,
> equal pay,
> dismissal from work.

For the area you have chosen, identify the following:

a the reason for the legislation being introduced,
b any groups or individuals involved in pressing for the changes,
c any opposition to the changes,
d the attitudes of the major political parties.

You will be required to report back orally to the rest of your group on your findings.

It may help you to talk to individuals who remember the introduction of these changes in order to obtain some idea from them of the social and political context. You will also need to carry out some research in the library identifying suitable material to help you to examine the legislative area chosen.

Collective labour law

In addition to changes in legislation affecting the rights of individual employees, there has also been considerable legislation affecting the rights of employees collectively. Collective labour law is concerned to a great extent with the way in which trade unions operate.

Trade unions are concerned with improving their members' terms and conditions of work, and to do this they direct their attention both to employers and to Government because the decisions of each affect trade unionists' living standards. An employee alone has very little power to influence an employer but, through their trade unions, employees are able to negotiate collectively with employers.

The main feature of collective labour law in this country is that it rests primarily on a framework of statutory immunities rather than positively stated legal rights. This means that laws have been passed which have exempted trade unions from conventional legal doctrines in order to allow them to function, rather than specifically setting out their rights.

In recent years there have been many changes in the law relating to trade unions. Some of the main areas affected have included:

Union recognition

Historically there has been no legal obligation on employers to recognize trade unions. If employers do recognize a trade union then it means that they are willing to negotiate with the officers of that union with regard to employees' pay, conditions, etc. Obviously if the employer refuses to recognize a union, then it is very difficult for that union to represent its members' interests. Under the 1975 Employment Protection Act, where employers refused to recognize trade unions, the union could appeal to the Advisory Conciliation and Arbitration Service (ACAS). ACAS provides an arena for the discussion of labour disputes. It attempts to encourage the voluntary settlement of disputes by bringing the two sides together with members of ACAS present. ACAS can only make recommendations; it does not have any powers to enforce its findings. In the case of an appeal to ACAS over union recognition under the 1975 Act, if ACAS recommended recognition but the employer refused, the union could unilaterally bring a claim on pay and conditions before the Central Arbitration Committee for a binding and enforceable arbitration award. The decision on pay and conditions would then have been binding on the employer.

The 1980 Employment Act removed the role of ACAS from trade union recognition disputes and left such disputes to be fought out at the place of work.

Trade union ballots

The 1984 Trade Union Act further removed protection from civil actions against trade unions where strikes or other industrial action are called or endorsed by a union without a preceding ballot of the members. This means that if a strike takes place without a ballot then the employer concerned could take the union to court and make a claim against them for financial loss due to the strike. If a ballot of members is taken prior to the strike then no such action could be taken by the employer.

Employers have been quite reluctant to bring legal actions against trade unions which they recognize and negotiate with, partly because taking such action might be counter-productive, possibly deepening the dispute or potentially souring relationships after the immediate dispute has been settled.

Picketing

The legal right to picket (that is, to communicate information peacefully and to persuade in the circumstances of a trade dispute) was established in the 1870s and is regarded by trade unionists as an essential part of ensuring the effectiveness of a strike.

The law on picketing was modified by the 1980 Employment Act following the widespread use of 'flying pickets' (pickets who moved about the country picketing other places of work) and mass **secondary picketing**. These tactics were used effectively in the 1974 miners' strike. Miners moved about the country picketing electricity generating stations and coal distribution depots; this was secondary picketing because they were not just picketing their own place of work and their own employer. Such action was effective because the miners were able to reduce the delay before the strike affected customers; lack of coal at the generating stations caused widespread power cuts.

The 1980 Act confined lawful picketing to employees or former employees (and associated union officials) picketing at their own place of employment or the place from which their work is managed, eg a head office. Secondary picketing is therefore unlawful. However, enforcement does not rest with the police but with those affected by the secondary picketing, eg the employer. At the same time as the change in the law, a Department of Employment Code of Practice set out a number of guidelines for picketing, including the suggested limit of six pickets at each entrance to a place of work. This measure was designed to eliminate the use of mass picketing; it is not however a legal limit but only a recommendation.

The 1980 Employment Act also imposed restrictions on the use of sympathetic industrial action, eg where members of one union take industrial action in support of members of another union who are in dispute.

Activity 5	If there is a major industrial dispute occurring at present, try to find out as much as possible about the causes of the dispute and the legal implications of it. You will need to read newspaper articles and to watch and listen to news items on the matter. Write a summary explaining in what ways the law on employment and trade unions has been involved in the dispute.

The picket line in a union recognition dispute.

Conclusion

These are just some aspects of the detailed legislation which surrounds the area of industrial relations and the relationship between employer and employee. Coupled with the law relating to the individual employee which you also examined in detail in this block, you should now be aware of the major changes which have taken place in this area and of the reasons for those changes.

Summary of skills

The intention of the study involved in this unit is not only to learn facts about organizations, but also to develop skills which will be of use in the business world. This section at the end of each block of work is to indicate the skills areas you should have developed during each activity.

Skills

Skill	Activities in which skill is developed
a Learning and studying	All activities
b Communicating	All activities
c Identifying and tackling problems	2, 4
d Information gathering	2, 3, 4
e Working with others	2, 3, 4
f Numeracy	4

Links with other units

You should also appreciate the links which exist between your studies in this area and your studies of *People in Organizations* and *Finance*. These activities are related to the acquisition and use of information which you will undertake as part of the *People in Organizations* unit. In the *Finance* unit the financial implications of human and legal pressures may be considered.

Block 7
Production, Technology and Change

Introduction

In this block of work we examine different production
processes and you are asked to identify the processes used in
firms in your locality. We then look closely at the
production of newspapers and at the implications of changes
in the production process. This will entail your gaining an
understanding of the techniques used in the newspaper
industry and of the new technology which is available.

Production processes

Every production process can be regarded as unique, whether
it involves a craft, such as a potter moulding clay at a wheel,
or robots on an assembly line producing cars.

Production is the activity which converts raw materials into
manufactured goods. The machines, the materials and the
people involved, can be organized in a number of different
ways. We now need to examine the various production
processes in more detail.

Although the methods of production will be looked at
separately, it should be remembered that it is commonplace
to find examples of, or combinations of, any two or three in
use under one roof.

Three main types of production can be distinguished.

Flow production

Flow production
(electric cookers).

This system is a form of mass production and is frequently associated with assembly work where large volumes are involved.

The items produced in this manner tend to be standardized, because of the complexities of production planning. Operatives working on such a production line tend to perform short work cycles, performing the same actions again and again. The work force tends to be unskilled or semi-skilled, apart from the engineers who set up the line and maintain it. In order to ensure continuous production, there must be a pool of adequately trained personnel to cover for absenteeism or personal needs (which may mean that work stations are temporarily uncovered).

Most mass-production lines will be computerized to some extent. In recent years, there has been a move towards robotic production, where machines are increasingly used to perform some of the more repetitive work. The modern car assembly plant is a good example of mass production making use of robotics.

Because of the enormous investment involved in setting up a flow production line, a regular demand for the product is vital in order to recover the costs involved and to give an adequate return on investment. If orders fall below the level of output, then it is normal to build up stocks rather than reduce output.

Batch production

This method is usually confined to situations where the demand for the item is insufficient to allow mass production methods to operate efficiently. It involves the manufacture of a product in small or large quantities, by a series of operations where the entire batch is completed in one operation before the next one is started. This system is common in the engineering industry.

The disadvantages involved in this type of production are the waste of resources and time involved, as only one item in the batch can be processed at any one time. This means that at any particular point in time, most items are either waiting to be processed or waiting to proceed to the next operation. One of the problems for the manufacturer is to decide what is an economic run. It may be very difficult to minimize costs per unit on the size of production run required by customers. On the other hand, if the quantity produced is in excess of immediate requirements, the extra amount produced will have to be stored, and this will incur storage charges.

Batch production (compact disks).

Jobbing production

This method of production involves work being carried out to the specific requirements of the individual customer. Engineering components designed to meet the specifications of individual customers would be produced in this manner. Aircraft construction too would involve this type of organization.

Such production methods involve a great deal of technical expertise on the part of the worker. Since the emphasis is on craft skill rather than quantity, this type of work tends to have higher labour costs and to provide greater job satisfaction.

Jobbing production (pool tables).

The production process may be considered as the ultimate management test, requiring the co-ordination of people, machines, materials, information, orders and stock. A change in any one of these variables will have an impact on all the others.

Unit and small batch production, as we have already seen, is normally carried out by more highly skilled workers. As more and more of the same good is demanded, it becomes cheaper to manufacture by mass production, with each individual worker assembling part of the finished product.

With some products and with the increasing applications of computers to the production field, process production becomes a viable alternative. Automated processing has been used for some time now in the petro-chemical industry and is also being applied to food processing and car manufacture. The main feature of this production method is the elimination of the production worker as machinery becomes the prime producer. People are instead involved in the programming and maintenance of the machinery.

These differences in production processes and in the application of technology account for many variations in organization structure. Automated plants, for example, tend to have a high proportion of administrative and managerial personnel compared with production operatives. In contrast, assembly line production is identified by a large proportion of direct production operatives.

Activity 1	In order for you to get a clearer idea of the distinction between the different production methods described above, you should now examine production in some of the firms situated in your locality.

Take three or more local firms and obtain information (possibly by a visit) on the production processes involved. Categorize them into flow, batch or jobbing production.

When you have completed your local investigations, you can move on to examine one particular area of production and technology in more detail.

In the case which follows, you are provided with information on the newspaper industry. The information details the production processes in use and the changes in technology which are taking place. It is written from the point of view of a printworker discussing the changes which have taken place or which are likely to take place within the industry.

New technology – News technology

There has been enormous pressure at all newspapers to change production processes and invest in new technology. New techniques are available in all production departments but the main focus of attention of new investment is in the composing process and plate-making area. Management within the industry argue that costs have risen over recent years due to the trebling of newsprint costs since 1970, increased competition within the industry, and rising labour costs. They say that something must be done to reduce costs and the answer is to be new technology.

The 'hot-metal' method

In order to understand what is happening to processes in the newspaper industry you have to understand something about its history.

The composition of modern newspapers at speed was really made possible with the invention of the Linotype machine. The first one was installed at the *New York Tribune* in 1886.

A Linotype machine and compositor.

This was the 'hot–metal' system; of course it's still used by many newspapers. The reporter writes the article and the copy is sub-edited. The copy is then set by operators sitting at the keyboards of Linotype machines. These produce slugs of type, a line at a time from molten alloy. Headlines are added to the columns of type which are assembled by hand in metal frames by the 'stonehand'. One frame for each page. An impression of the finished page is then cast into a semi–cylindrical plate, which is then bolted on to a rotary letterpress printing machine.

In some places this process has been eliminated by photocomposition.

Photocomposition

In some newspapers where this is used, every word printed is typed twice, once by the journalist on to paper and then by the compositor.

The compositor operates a machine similar to a large electric typewriter, which sets the word as punched tape. This is fed into a computer which hyphenates the copy and sets the margins. It is then switched to a photosetter which works at the rate of 3000 lines a minute and turns out the type as artwork on photographic paper. A Linotype operator who has to use his own eye to hyphenate produces only 6000 letters an hour.

The columns of type are then cut to size with a scalpel and pasted up to make a page. The completed pages are photographed and put through a photo-engraving machine to be made into plates before being fixed to the presses.

Even more advanced technology than this is available and is about to be introduced.

The latest technology

With the latest process and computer applications, compositors type onto computer keyboards, the typed words are stored on a computer disk and transferred directly via a cathode ray tube and camera onto photographic paper.

Journalists
composing by an
electronic system
in a regional
newspaper.

Of course, there's really no need for the compositor to
do the typing; the words can be fed into the computer
directly by the reporter sitting at a visual display unit.
The keyboard can be linked to a television screen which
not only shows what has been typed but also how much
space the article will take up in the paper. The results of
this can be sub-edited and corrected without anything
appearing on paper. With the press of a key the
reporter's work can be fed into the computer and set
within seconds without anyone else being involved in
the operation.

The articles and advertisements in Eddie Shah's new
national tabloid newspaper *Today* are written and edited
on computer terminals and 'laid-out' into pages on
electronic screens. The illustrations and graphics are also
created on computer screens all without the work of a
single compositor, 'stone-hand' or process worker. The
result of this work is fully made-up pages which can be
sent electronically to five regional printing centres. The
papers are printed and then distributed by road using
local firms operating under a franchise.

Shah reckons he can produce his paper with 800 people and cover his costs if he obtains a circulation of 300 000. The *Daily Telegraph* and *Sunday Telegraph* have 1900 production workers in London and more in Manchester: quite a difference in numbers.

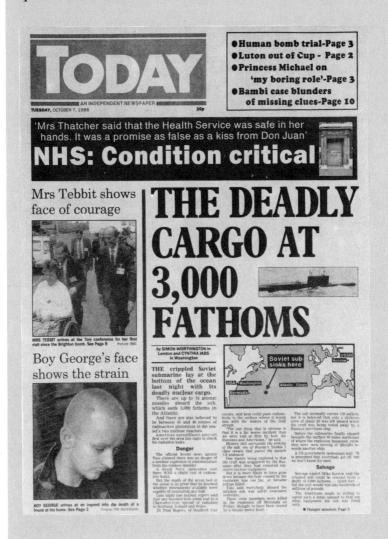

The front page of the *Today* newspaper.

Changing technology

In newspapers there are three clear stages. Firstly linotype machines, which require skilled operators, are replaced by computer typesetting. Secondly this typing is no longer done by printers at all but by journalists and other personnel taking advertisements over the telephone. Thirdly the journalists' work itself is revolutionized as the layout of the newspaper is completed on a visual display unit. At each stage a new group of workers bears the burden of the technological change.

Of course there are drawbacks to this new technology apart from the job losses. For example, direct input from journalists is very suitable for a lightly sub-edited newspaper. Many of the papers in Britain are not lightly sub-edited. Also although such direct input offers a huge saving on labour, it doesn't necessarily save time, because of the difficulty of sub-editing.

Take a look at the American newspapers: they've introduced new technology but the quality of the papers has declined. Editors can buy ready-produced stories from press agencies and at the press of a computer key they can be set in the paper without even having been read.

Trade union attitudes

Basically the unions have been wary of the introduction of new technology, whether it's been intermediate technology using photocomposition or the more drastic on-line system incorporating direct input by journalists. The main problem is job losses. Of course, it's OK to oppose compulsory redundancies, but accepting voluntary redundancies or natural wastage means less jobs available for school leavers. Shorter working hours are one way of maintaining jobs, but that's usually opposed by management due to the cost implications.

In some ways, of course, the union response is made more complicated because of the separate print unions on the production side. This means that when new technology is introduced and there are changes in working practices, disputes can arise over who does the new work, a member of one union, or of another.

The introduction of a photocomposition system would affect those workers involved in the composing process and in plate-making. It would mean the end of the traditional skills of the Linotype operators (compositors) and the stonehands (those responsible for making up the pages). The printers' objections are very simple: they see these changes as a scale of automation which will not only obliterate skills but decimate jobs as well.

The provincial newspapers in this country have already modernized to a certain extent. That led to a big shake-out of printers, particularly compositors. Between 1967 and 1976 there was a loss of 63 000 jobs in the printing industry. Most of the jobs lost were those of skilled craftsmen and were the direct result of new technology.

From the information above you can clearly identify the traditional technology still used in the newspaper industry. The traditional 'hot-metal' process can be represented by the diagram shown below.

Flow chart for the hot-metal process.

| *Activity 2* | Using information from the case-study produce two simple flow charts, one for photocomposition and one for direct input. |

| *Activity 3* | Using the two flowcharts which you have just produced and the one showing the hot-metal process, identify the points where the major changes in process take place. What changes in working practices will occur? Which skills will be lost and which jobs threatened? |

Check your answers against the information given at the end of the block.

| *Activity 4* | Write a short article explaining, from the point of view of management, why it is so essential to make use of the new technology in the newspaper industry. |

Your article will need to deal with the following factors:
1 the need to reduce unit costs in order to retain profitability,
2 the effect of rising newsprint costs,
3 the effect of rising labour costs,
4 the problem of declining circulation and increasing competition.

| *Activity 5* | When new technology is introduced, why do you think conflict may arise between management and workforce? If you were a trade union representative for print workers who were about to be affected by the introduction of new technology at their place of work, what issues would you wish to raise with management? Check your work for this activity with the guidance given at the end of the block. |

Recent developments in the newspaper industry

Fleet Street, the home of national newspapers, has in 1986 gone through some major changes. The launch of *Today* saw a new national newspaper coming on the scene, and the movement of Rupert Murdoch's *News International* titles (including *The Times* and the *Sun*) from Fleet Street to Wapping caused a major industrial dispute involving both the NGA and SOGAT.

The News
International
Building at
Wapping.

Management within the newspaper industry has pointed to the major financial problems facing the business. Costs of both newsprint and labour have been too high: papers like *The Times* and the *Sun* have been employing too many people for the turnover achieved, and this has meant low profits and therefore a lack of investment to develop the business. Nearly all the major national papers have therefore had to look at the possibilities offered by new technology.

Rupert Murdoch decided in the late 1970s to look at the possibilities provided by a move from Fleet Street to the docklands. In negotiations with the unions they pressed to maintain the sorts of terms and conditions which they had enjoyed in Fleet Street, and to apply them to work at Wapping. At the end of 1985 Murdoch set a Christmas deadline for the agreement of the unions to his plans for shifting production to Wapping. His requirements included that the unions recognize the management's absolute right to manage, that there should be no closed shop (where all workers must be members of a union), and that the unions should adhere to a legally binding agreement including a 'no-strike' clause.

The trade unions rejected Murdoch's document on the basis that it negated the possibility of taking industrial action. The union's members on Fleet Street papers were then given six months' notice. The unions balloted their members for industrial action and in February 1986 began picketing Rupert Murdoch's new plant at Wapping which was manned by other workers and which already had the presses rolling.

Trade unions

The National Graphical Association banner.

As has already been mentioned, there were a number of trade unions representing printworkers. They included:

1 National Graphical Association (NGA)   This union represents craftworkers, mainly from the areas of composing, processing and foundry work.
2 Society of Lithographic Artists, Designers and Engravers (SLADE)   This union represents craftworkers in processing.
3 Society of Graphical and Allied Trades (SOGAT)   This union represents noncraft workers.
4 National Society of Operative Printers, Graphical and Media Personnel (NATSOPA)   Representing ancillary and clerical workers within the printing industry.

Of these four unions, the NGA and SLADE have now amalgamated as have SOGAT and NATSOPA. The major differences between the two amalgamated unions is the strong craft outlook of the NGA and the broader industrial view of SOGAT.

The earliest unions were craft unions which were formed to control the number of entrants to a particular trade. In order to be a member of a trade union an individual had to practise that particular craft. Very few wholly craft unions exist today however.

Later, general unions were formed which took as their members the semi-skilled and unskilled workers. The members did not have to have a particular skill and worked in many different areas. Examples of general unions today include the Transport and General Workers Union (TGWU) and the National Union of Public Employees (NUPE).

Some workers organized on an industry basis, regardless of the type of work or skills involved. Examples of industrial unions in Britain include the National Union of Mineworkers and the Iron and Steel Trades Confederation. The biggest growth in trade union membership in recent years has ocurred in white-collar work, including representation of workers in local government by the National Association of Local Government Officers (NALGO) and teachers by the National Union of Teachers (NUT), as well as many others.

Functions of trade unions

Regardless of the type of trade union, the major function of any union is to protect its members' interests whether they are skilled workers with a particular craft, or unskilled workers.

Employers and employees may have different and sometimes conflicting interests. This does not mean that there are continual disagreements but that each may have different needs and may perceive the same situation differently. We have already seen in our study of the newspaper industry that management wants to introduce new technology in order to increase efficiency and reduce costs, whereas the workers recognize the threat to skills and jobs which such action would entail.

Trade unions are concerned with improving their members' terms and conditions of work and generally with improving the quality of life of working people.

Objectives of trade unions

The objectives which trade unions generally set themselves
include some or all of the following:

1 Improved conditions of employment: this includes better
   pay for members, shorter hours and longer holidays, better
   maternity and sickness provision.
2 An improved physical environment at work: this may
   mean ensuring there is adequate heating, lighting and
   ventilation, also actively ensuring that the Health and
   Safety at Work Act 1974 is adhered to (you will examine
   this in detail in *People in Organizations 2*).
3 Greater job security: this includes trying to reduce the
   numbers of closures or redundancies by negotiation or
   industrial action, as well as acting for members in cases of
   unfair dismissal.
4 The promotion of job satisfaction and job prospects for
   members: this may involve,   *a* negotiation of training
   and retraining programmes for members, particularly
   where de-skilling is occurring and members' traditional
   skills are being replaced by automation and are therefore
   no longer required and,   *b* the promotion of equal
   opportunities within workplaces.
5 Achievement of income security: this includes ensuring the
   protection of income when work is interrupted by illness,
   accident, old age, redundancy or unemployment.
6 Improvements in general standard of living, involving
   pressing for better provision of education, health care and
   housing.
7 Defence of trade unions' rights to operate freely: this may
   involve opposition to legislation designed to curb trade
   unions' rights.

Of course the main characteristic of a trade union is that its
representatives bargain collectively on behalf of its members.
This process of collective bargaining on matters of pay,
conditions, redundancies, etc, means that instead of each
worker trying to bargain alone with the management, the
union represents the members' collective views.

Organization of trade unions

Every union has its own particular pattern of organization
but, in general, most are structured in a pyramid fashion.

A trade union organizational pyramid.

At the base of the pyramid are all the members of the union. Within each workplace the members will elect a workplace representative, sometimes called a **shop steward**, or **union represenatative**. They are not paid by the union, and combine union business with their own work. It is their job to act as the members' spokesperson in negotiations or dealings with management.

Individual members will be organized into local branches. A local union branch may draw its members from several different firms in the area or be based on one workplace. Branch meetings discuss local issues and elect representatives to the district committee and to attend the annual national conference of their union. Most unions have a yearly conference, at which important issues concerning union policy will be discussed and any decisions taken will then be acted on by the executive committee.

Printing and unions

Craft traditions have tended to dominate in printing and the print unions maintain the old 'chapel' structure. The chapel is the basic workshop organization and historically the chapels have had great autonomy. In some cases the printing chapels are responsible for recruitment and control of overtime rates; these would in other industries be the responsibility of management.

Printing has long had a strong labour organization in both skilled and semi-skilled work. The craft workers in particular have been able to exert some measure of control over their working conditions.

Type composition is being taken over by the combination of typing the word and setting the type. Technology is being used to break up the sequence of work into simplified areas. By placing the emphasis on volume production, technology is facilitating the introduction of mass production methods into composition.

The unions representing compositors tend to accept the inevitability of computer-based systems, but demand that control of the inputting remains in their hands. This leads to problems where nonprint-union staff are also inputting by keyboard but have poorer wages and conditions than print-union members.

So how should the print unions react to the introduction of new technology? The diagram below attempts to represent the first stage of a possible negotiating process.

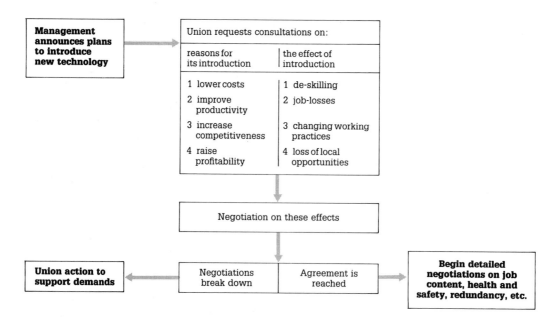

The negotiation process.

Activity 6

Faced with the introduction of new technology and the resulting job losses, de-skilling and loss of local employment opportunities, what suggestions could the union make to alleviate these problems?

Naturally, the unions' suggestions to cope with the introduction of new technology may not meet the approval of management, although they may serve the immediate interests of union members.

Union aim	Achieved by
1 No reduction in the total workforce, therefore no compulsory or voluntary redundancies.	A shorter working week, retraining of workforce, expansion of the firm's output, blacking of new technology.
2 No reduction in local employment opportunities.	Maintaining the existing workforce and not allowing natural wastage to reduce manpower.

If the introduction of new techology is designed to reduce costs and increase profitability then a shorter working week for employees will not be an attractive alternative for management as this will simply maintain labour costs, not reduce them.

If the firm is intending to expand output in conjunction with the introduction of new technology, then jobs need not be affected.

Faced with the possibility of unions blacking the introduction of new technology and thus preventing its use to lower costs, management may consider it feasible in the short-term to allow a shorter working week or the maintenance of employment levels above those strictly necessary.

Apart from the conflict which might arise due to possible job losses, it seems that many people within business organizations, not only trade union members, are suspicious of change.

Resistance to change

We have already identified some of the reasons for resistance to change, eg job losses, loss of skill, and changes in working practices. Other factors which may cause resistance include:
1 changes in status
2 inconvenience and disruption
3 the threat of uncertainty,
4 lack of control.

Apart from the direct negotiations between trade unions and management which we have already examined, management may also seek to alleviate the resistance to change by other methods.

Activity 7	What suggestions can you make for overcoming the resistance to change which management can expect to face on the introduction of new technology?

The exact methods of overcoming resistance to change will depend upon the nature of the changes but may include some of the following:
1 Offering financial incentives, for example redundancy settlements and increased pay for operating new machinery.
2 Ensuring sufficient training for personnel involved in the changes.
3 Introducing changes on a trial basis.
4 Introducing changes gradually, working up to major innovations.
5 Ensuring that the workforce is consulted fully.
6 Allowing workers' representatives to participate in decision–making.

Conclusion

Whatever may be the answer to the introduction of a specific piece of new technology, it should be clear from the work completed in this block that changing production processes may give rise to conflict. Inevitably management will look at new technology from the point of view of cost-saving and increased profitability, whereas the workforce and particular individuals may see it as a threat to their livelihood. The problem which organizations face is how to deal with such difficulties in order that production can continue uninterrupted.

Guidance for Activity 3

In a move from the hot-metal method to photo-composition the major changes which would take place would include:
1 a move from the use of Linotype operated by a skilled operator producing solid lines of type to computer typesetting,
2 the loss of the skills of the linotype operator who uses his own eye to hyphenate and justify, and the loss of the skills of the 'stonehand' setting the type into the metal frame,
3 the jobs most threatened are those of the Linotype operator and the 'stonehand'.

In moving to the direct input method of production, the major changes which would take place would include:
1 a move towards the reporter directly in-putting copy onto computer tape, the page being designed on the computer screen,
2 the loss of skills mainly concerns the elimination of the need for pasting up the pages,
3 the jobs most threatened are those of printers who previously typed copy onto the computer keyboard and those who pasted up the pages.

Guidance for Activity 5

The concern of a trade union is to represent the interests of its members. Bearing that in mind, the sorts of issues which you would want to have raised in Activity 5 should have included:
1 the problems of de-skilling,
2 job losses,
3 redundancies,
4 loss of employment opportunities,
5 rising productivity and the beneficiaries of this.

Summary of skills

The intention of the study involved in this unit is not only to learn facts about organizations, but also to develop skills which will be of use in the business world. This section at the end of each block of work is to indicate the skills areas you should have developed during each activity.

Skills

Skill	*Activities in which skill is developed*
a Working with others	1, 4, 5
b Information gathering	1
c Learning and studying	All activities
d Identifying and tackling problems	1, 6, 7
e Communicating	1, 2, 4, 6, 7
f Information processing	3, 4, 5, 6, 7
g Design and visual discrimination	2

Links with other units

You should also appreciate the links which exist between your studies in this area and your studies of *People in Organizations* and *Finance*. These activities are related to electronic technology and communication which you will examine as part of the *People in Organizations* unit. In the *Finance* unit the examination of costs in relation to decision-making and the wider implications of financial decisions would provide an appreciation of financial objectives in relation to technological change.

Block 8
Marketing

Introduction

This block of work is designed to help you to examine the marketing function of business organizations. The focus of marketing is the potential customers for the organization's products. In order to be able to plan effectively, any organization needs information on the likely demand for its products, the pattern of sales over time, and the factors which cause consumers to buy one firm's products in preference to another.

In order to examine the various elements of the marketing function we shall look at the fast food market, which has grown considerably over recent years, selling anything from chickens and burgers to pizzas and ice-cream. The work in this block will involve you in an examination of fast food outlets in your locality and in the production of a detailed report combining your own observations with marketing theory.

The fast food market

Looking around the centre of any large town or city you cannot fail to notice an increasing number of fast food outlets. Some of the well-known names include McDonalds, Wimpey, Kentucky Fried Chicken, Spud–U–Like, etc.

Activity 1	Working in groups of two or three, go into your local town centre and find out where the fast food outlets are. Some of the outlets may be well known nationally, while others will be local businesses.
	Identify on a local map the location of fast food outlets in the area of examination. How competitive is the fast food market in your local area?

If you have chosen to examine fast food outlets in a city centre then you may well have found a number of different outlets operating in close proximity.

Mintel, the market research company, suggests that 'fast food offers an excellent opportunity for companies established in other fields to diversify, and the market seems to thrive on competition' (*Financial Times*, 7 October 1985). It argues that four or five different types of fast food outlets can operate in close proximity, creating a form of fast food centre and drawing more business to the area, which means increased sales for all of the outlets in that area.

The implication is that the market for fast food is a highly competitive market with a large number of relatively small outlets competing against one another in order to sell their particular product. Each outlet will therefore have a relatively small share of the total market.

Market types

The markets for the supply of different products can be identified in terms of the degree of competition present. It is usual to refer to four different major market forms.

1 Competitive market

In a competitive market, many suppliers compete, each supplier having a relatively small share of the market.

2 Imperfectly competitive market

In an imperfectly competitive market, many suppliers sell products which, although basically the same in their characteristics and eventual usage, do have a degree of product differentiation, eg only ICI produce Dulux paint but there are many other similar paints on the market.

3 Oligopoly

There is an oligopoly in a market when there are very few suppliers of a product. This usually occurs where the take-over and merger of companies has resulted in the manufacture of a product being heavily concentrated in a few very large companies, eg detergents are largely produced by Proctor and Gamble, and Unilever.

What types of market do the products in these photographs represent?

4 *Monopoly*

There is a monopoly in a market when one supplier controls the supply of a particular product. Legislation governing monopolies allows, however, for the investigation of mergers where 25% of the total market would be controlled by one supplier. Such a degree of control gives the monopolist the ability to determine the price he will sell his product for or the quantity which he wishes to sell.

Markets for different types of goods and services can also be divided up according to who the purchaser is likely to be.

1 *Consumer markets*

In consumer markets, goods and services are purchased for final consumption without undergoing any further transactions. The UK consumer market consists of approximately 56 million consumers and its total value amounted to £182 427 million in 1983. The proportion spent on food was 14.9%, a value of £27 148 million.

2 *Industrial markets*

In industrial markets, goods and services are purchased by companies involved in the production of other goods which are then sold to other manufacturers or to final consumers, eg raw materials, steel.

3 *Distribution markets*

In distribution markets, goods are bought by those involved in their distribution, such as retailers and wholesalers.

4 *Government markets*

In government markets, goods and services are sold to local authorities and central government.

Activity 2 Using the list of local fast food outlets which you identified in Activity 1, identify the form of ownership for each outlet. Some local businesses may be operating as sole traders, other national outlets may be franchises. When you have identified the different forms of ownership, read through the next section.

You may have identified a number of different types of ownership operating in the fast food outlets which you examined as part of Activity 2. Most of these should have been familiar to you from the work carried out in Block 2; in addition, one form of ownership and organization which you probably identified amongst fast food outlets is franchising.

Franchising

Franchising in the UK began with brewers who created the tied house system to guarantee outlets for their beer. It has developed mainly in the motor trade, through franchised petrol stations, car dealers, and spare parts dealers. The new areas for franchising tend to be the fast food, servicing and retail sectors.

Franchising is where a company establishes a contractual relationship with owners of separate businesses which operate under the franchisor's name in a specified manner to market a product or service. The franchise company (the franchisor) makes available to an independent trader (the franchisee) the know-how, equipment, materials and rights to a nationally advertised trade name. For the franchisee the main advantage is the benefit of operating in an area where the business and clientèle are already established.

The franchisee normally buys the franchise by paying over a lump sum to the franchisor. A continuing royalty is then paid, which can either be a percentage of the turnover, or a surcharge on the cost of the basic supplies. This royalty covers the cost of local and national advertising, administrative back-up and advice and further training.

The amount of money needed to obtain a franchise varies considerably. The British Franchise Association suggests that the outlay required from a franchisee is on average £26 000 per unit. A much larger amount would have to be paid for an outlet in a prime location. The major banks have responded to the growth in franchising by setting up specialist departments to check out franchisors and to offer financial packages for potential franchisees.

Members of the British Franchising Association

FULL MEMBERS of the British Franchising Association are required to have operated a successful pilot scheme for one year and to have at least four franchises, two of whom must have been franchising for at least two years.

AT Computer World. Sale of microcomputers and computer supplies.

Accounting Centre. Computerised accounting services and "company doctor" service.

ANC. Next-day nationwide parcel freight delivery and collection service.

Anicare Group Services (Veterinary). Management services to the veterinary profession.

AP Autela. Automotive part suppliers.

Apollo Window Blinds. Retail franchise—supply of fashion window blinds and associated services.

Badgeman. Manufacture and sale of personal name badges.

A. F. Blakemore and Son. Convenience store.

Budget Rent-a-car International. Self-drive car, van and truck rental service.

Burgerking (UK). Fast food restaurants.

BSM City Link Transport. Same-day and overnight parcel delivery service.

Colour Counsellors. Colour catalogued samples of wallpapers, carpets and fabrics.

Command Performance. Ladies and men's hairdressing.

Computerland. Retail sale of microcomputer software and hardware.

Conder Clentech. Industrial and commercial ceiling and wall-cleaning specialists.

Davenports Brewery. Retail distribution of beers, wines, spirits and minerals to the home.

Dyno-Rod. Drain and pipe-cleaning service.

Extract from the directory of members of the British Franchising Association.

Franchising can remove some of the uncertainty which many small businessmen face while providing many of the rewards, eg job satisfaction and the financial advantages of self-employment. The number of UK franchisees dealing with reputable franchisors which fail each year is relatively small, about 2 per cent. The failure rate for small businesses is much higher. The high success rate of franchises is probably due to the personal motivation of the franchisee and the guidance and back-up from the franchising company.

For the franchising company, the system offers an easy way of expanding rapidly with limited financial and managerial resources. Most of the development capital is put up by the franchisee and the motivation of franchisees is high, owing to their independence.

Some of the more familiar areas where franchising operates
include the following:

McDonalds	—	*Fast food*
Burger King	—	
Wimpy	—	
Spud–U–Like	—	
Dyno–Rod	—	*Drain & pipe cleaning*
Metro–Rod	—	
Silver Shield	—	*Windscreen replacement service*
Highway Windscreens	—	
Prontaprint	—	*Instant printing service*
Kall–Kwik Printing	—	
The Body Shop	—	*Cosmetics and Toiletries*
Benetton	—	*Clothing*
Phildar	—	
Pronuptia	—	
Tie Rack	—	

Activity 3	Using your list of fast food outlets, identify the range of products which the various outlets offer for sale.

Product planning

All firms rely on the sales of their products to produce
sufficient revenue to create a profit. In order to ensure that
this is happening, firms need to examine how well their
products fit consumer needs, the extent of competition and
changing market and product trends.

The product

The products of many companies are tangible goods which
are consumed, eg food and cars. However, a product may
also be intangible, as is the case with the output of service
industries, eg banking and insurance.

In today's very competitive marketing environment,
companies use a variety of different strategies to distinguish
their products from those of the competition.

Product differentiation is based on the assumption that customers will purchase a product for a variety of reasons. Customers may be attracted by design, colour, packaging or technical features; on a less tangible level they may be attracted by the image of the product and the reputation of the manufacturer.

The product, whether it is a good or a service, is made up of these features. It is the function of marketing to assess what the customer wants from the product and to combine these wants to offer the most attractive product.

Activity 4 | Take two of the fast food outlets with which you are familiar and which are in direct competition. Discuss the methods which they use to distinguish their products from their competitors'.

Product life cycle

Marketing is based on the assumption that all products have a life cycle. The product is introduced and begins to sell; the sales reach a peak and may stabilize for a period, but eventually start to decline. The product life cycle then consists of four stages: introduction, growth, maturity and decline.

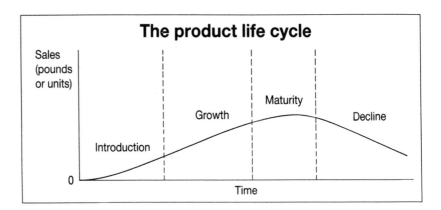

All products will follow this four-stage cycle, but the length of each phase varies depending on the nature of the product, marketing policies adopted, changes in technology, and competition.

During the introduction of a new product, sales tend to be low and demand increases slowly, as few people are aware of the new product. Many products fail to get past this stage, either because they have not anticipated the market or because the costs of the launch are too great for the limited financial resources of the firm.

Sales of a product will begin to 'take-off' as more people learn of it from advertising and promotion, and from those who have already purchased it. This is the growth stage.

Eventually sales will stabilize because the product has been purchased by the majority of those willing and able to do so. A high proportion of sales then consists of repeat purchases. As soon as this happens, competition intensifies as each firm attempts to maintain its market share.

Firms will try to retain their share of the market by employing **extension strategies**, which may include any of the following:
1 Development of new uses for existing products. Nylon is an ideal example of a product of which the life cycle was extended. It was originally employed primarily for military applications, in particular for parachutes, thread and rope. It was developed as a fabric and expanded into the clothing and hosiery market, and has also been used in tyre manufacture.
2 Modification of products in the light of technical changes, eg hi-fi equipment.
3 Development of styling changes which demonstrate the newness of the product, eg changes in the various models produced by car manufacturers.
4 Development of new markets for an existing product by modifying it to suit the requirements of the new market, eg developments in the computer field have expanded the market to include households and small firms.

Finally, sales of a product will begin to decline as a result of the introduction of new improved products or changes in consumer tastes.

Fashion goods may have a relatively short product life cycle, some items only being fashionable for perhaps one season. Other goods may have a much longer product life cycle, for example one model of car which has had a very long life cycle is the British Leyland Mini, first produced in the 1960s and still in production. Of course, modifications and design changes have produced minor alterations, but basically the Mini lives on.

| Activity 5 | Fast food outlets provide a service. Taking the fast food service in general, identify the stage which you think the service has reached in the product life cycle. Explain why you think that the fast food service has reached this particular stage. |

The product life cycle clearly indicates differing levels of demand for a product over time. For a company, demand and sales forecasting is important in order for the organization to be able to determine the overall scale of its operations.

Demand

The market demand for a product is the amount that could be purchased per year within a defined geographical area. The market potential for a product recognizes that with an increased marketing effort, it would be possible to persuade more people to buy.

A firm will need to understand the factors underlying demand for its products for a number of reasons:
1 in order to maintain or increase the firm's share of the total market,
2 to identify opportunities for new products,
3 in order to be able to plan ahead, an indication of future demand is necessary.

Factors affecting demand

With most products and services, it is usual to find that the higher the price of the product then the less will be demanded by consumers. Alternatively, if the price of a product falls, then we would expect buyers to buy more, or new consumers to be attracted to the product.

The relationship between the price of the product and the quantity demanded can be simply illustrated by the use of a graph.

Let's assume that a company producing video recorders estimates that they could sell varying numbers of recorders in a month if they charged different prices. This information could be shown numerically in a table:

Price	Quantity of recorders demanded (per month)
£450	1000
£400	2500
£350	4000
£300	5000
£250	6500

This information can also be presented in graphical form by plotting the quantity of video recorders demanded against price.

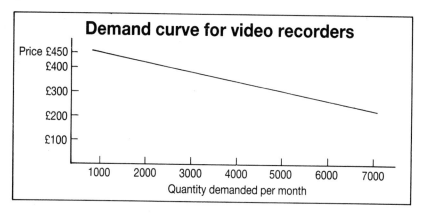

From the graph you can see that the demand curve slopes downwards from left to right, illustrating that at a higher price, smaller quantities are demanded and at a lower price greater quantities are demanded, eg at a price of £400, 2500 video recorders are demanded. If the price fell to £250 then demand would rise to 6500 units. A change in the price of the product then causes a movement along the curve.

Other factors which also affect the demand for a product actually cause a shift in the demand curve. Clearly consumers' tastes or preferences can change, causing a change in demand for a product. Take the skateboard craze; in the early 1970s skateboards were very popular and vast numbers of young people owned and used skateboards. In fact the craze soon died down; skateboards became less popular and sales fell. It is possible to show this change in demand on a diagram as at the top of the next page.

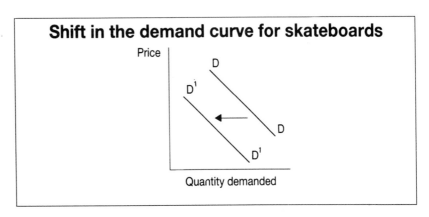

Shift in the demand curve for skateboards

Price

D

D¹

D

D¹

Quantity demanded

Let's assume that DD represents the demand for skateboards at the height of their popularity. When their popularity starts to decline, that can be represented by a shift in the demand curve to the left to D¹D¹. Demand curve D¹D¹ tells us that fewer skateboards will be bought at all the possible prices compared with the previous situation. The reverse (ie a shift to the right) would obviously occur if skateboards had become even more popular.

Variations in the level of consumers' incomes can also cause changes in the level of demand for a product. Assume that the Chancellor of the Exchequer in the budget abolished income tax for people earning £4000 per annum or less; this would have the effect of substantially increasing those people's incomes. One possible effect would be that these people might now be able to afford to eat more expensive cuts of meat, whereas previously they had bought sausages and mince. There could be an increase in the demand for, say, joints of beef.

Again this can be illustrated by the use of a diagram.

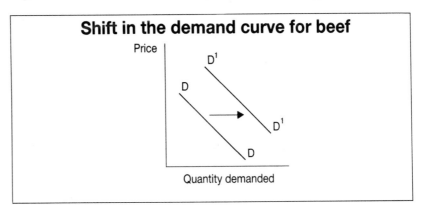

Shift in the demand curve for beef

Price

D¹

D

D¹

D

Quantity demanded

The demand curve DD represents the demand for beef prior to the tax changes which leave the lower paid with greater income levels. As people use their higher income to buy more beef, the demand curve shifts from DD to D^1D^1.

A change in the price of other goods can also affect the demand for particular products. Many goods have close substitutes, eg the Metro and the Vauxhall Nova are both small cars aimed at a similar market. If British Leyland decided to run a promotion campaign offering £750 off new Metros then it is likely that the demand for Metros would rise and the demand for Novas fall. People thinking of buying a new car would be attracted by the special offer on Metros.

Some goods are complementary to one another, ie the purchase of one leads to the purchase of the other. If the price of petrol rose substantially, thus increasing the costs of motoring, then the demand for cars is likely to fall.

Of course, changes in the population size and hence in the number of consumers, is also likely to have an effect on the demand for different goods.

Price-elasticity of demand

A factor which it is useful for a firm to consider is the price elasticity of demand for its product. This simply refers to the responsiveness of demand to a change in price, ie will a change in price affect the quantity demanded by a large or small amount?

Where demand or sales are unresponsive to price changes we say that demand for a product is **inelastic**, and where sales are highly responsive we say that demand for a product is **elastic**.

It is generally accepted that price-elasticity of demand for cigarettes is relatively inelastic. This means that the price can be increased without sales falling off too sharply.

One of the most valuable features of the concept of price-elasticity is that it gives the businessman some indication of what is likely to happen to the total revenue from sales of his product as a result of price changes. For example, if the price-elasticity of demand is elastic, total revenue from sales will fall in response to a price increase, because the increase in price (which could provide additional revenue) is offset by the reduction in sales. Conversely if price–elasticity of demand is inelastic, then total revenue from sales will rise in response to a price increase, because the adverse effect of the reduction in sales is more than offset by the price increase.

| Activity 6 | a The number of fast food outlets has been increasing over recent years, which must reflect a growth in the level of demand. Discuss the factors which you think explain this growth. |

a The number of fast food outlets has been increasing over recent years, which must reflect a growth in the level of demand. Discuss the factors which you think explain this growth.

b Now read the article below. Do you think its analysis is correct?

FAST LIVING — FAST FOOD

The reasons for the growth in fast-food catering in Britain are partly socio-economic but also arise from commercial pressures within the market, in particular the need for US companies to find somewhere to expand as their own market becomes saturated.

Changes in the make-up of the UK population and the growing importance of children, teenagers and the young family as consumers is also significant. Estimates suggest that while Britain's population has been slowly declining there is at present an increasing proportion of teenagers within it.

Increases in the number of teenagers in recent years are expected to push up the number of children born. Fast foods ingredients, speed, low cost, informality, all point to the under 25's as the target market.

Although households in Britain generally are getting smaller, the average household is gaining more collective spending power. In many there is more than one wage-earner, and this factor, as well as generating more disposable income, can also influence the extent of eating away from home, particularly when the additional breadwinner is the wife.

The effect of married women working on patterns of meal taking and food choice is considerable, tending to reduce the amount of communal meal taking and encouraging the use of fast and convenient food. Thus the use of take-away and competitively priced fast food outlets is encouraged.

The heavy marketing and promotional effort behind convenience food, particularly the TV advertising aimed at children, has helped to create acceptance for such products and has helped to condition consumers to snack-type meals.

Fast food's growing share of the eating-out market

Percentage shares of all meal occasions

	Year 1	Year 2	Year 3
Total number of meal occasions (millions)	311	315	335
Fast food/popular catering	%	%	%
Cafes and snack bars	12%	14%	15%
Takeaways	13%	14%	18%
Pub snacks	8%	9%	10%
In-store restaurants	2%	3%	3%
Hotels and restaurants	10%	10%	10%
Staff catering	44%	39%	31%
Schools, hospitals and institutional	11%	11%	13%

Market research

Marketing clearly involves a wide variety of decisions, from the particular market which a company should enter to changes in an old established product. Most business decision-making can be improved by having data relating to the market and the possible consequences of future market decisions. Market research is the term employed to embrace such information-collecting activities.

The purpose of market research is to gain insights into the nature and fabric of the market for a particular good or service.

Some of its specific applications are given below:
1 Gathering information to allow an analysis of the market: this may include measuring the total size of the market, by estimating who will buy the product, and how many people there are in that age group or income group.
2 Obtaining information to allow an analysis of sales: this may include taking past sales performance and using this to predict future sales, and looking at the share of the market taken by competitors.
3 Collecting information to allow an analysis of the product itself: this may include customer trials of new products to assess reactions, and investigation of how frequently the product is purchased and by whom.

Often a great deal of the information needed is already available within the organization, such as records of sales performance. Trade and technical journals and published material from independent market research agencies, such as Media Expenditure Analysis Limited (MEAL) which provides information on how much is spent by the different media and by whom, are sources of external information which may be useful to the marketing decision. The Government is also a major source of information, providing valuable detail through a variety of publications. Information on population can be obtained from the Census and Annual Abstract of Statistics. Income and expenditure levels, details on housing, manufactured goods and the structure of the retail trade, are just some of the areas covered by government publications.

The use of statistics which are already available is termed desk research. On the whole, a firm should only undertake its own survey or commission an agency to find out specific information if that information is important and is not available elsewhere. The cost of sending out questionnaires and carrying out surveys is high, and therefore should only be undertaken as a last resort.

Data collection

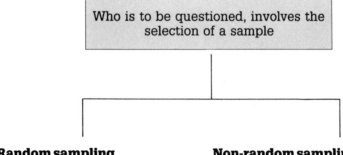

Sample selection.

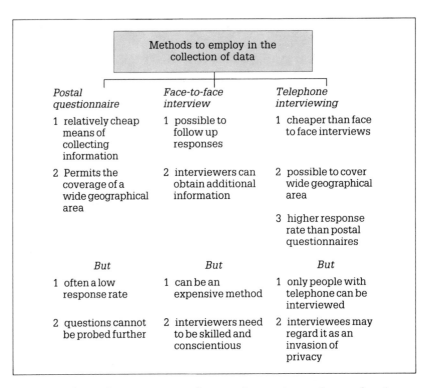

Data collection methods.

It is sound marketing research practice to investigate the data already available before embarking on any primary data collection.

If primary research is necessary, then one of the main methods of collecting information is by the use of a survey.

Before carrying out a survey the researcher has to decide upon who is to be questioned and how the questioning is to take place.

Questionnaire design

Obviously, if a questionnaire is to be administered then it must be well designed, otherwise the information required may not be forthcoming. Questionnaire design is an extensive subject in its own right; however, here are some points which need to be considered:
1 Ensure that the questions asked seek the information which is pertinent to the aims of the research.
2 The questions must be clear and easily understood by respondents.
3 The questions should not be phrased in such a way as to lead the respondent to give the desired response.

4 Choose a blend of different types of questions. Be aware of the advantages and disadvantages of using closed and open-ended questions. Closed questions include questions with Yes/No type answers and multiple choice questions where a respondent makes a selection from several alternatives. Open-ended questions allow the interviewee to respond in any way they want, and at some length. Responses to open-ended questions are usually more difficult to analyse than those given in response to closed questions.

The example given below illustrates the range of questions possible and provides some indication of layout.

Survey of facilities for students at Ashcroft College of Further Education

This questionnaire has been compiled in order to discover students' views about college facilities and how these might be improved.

Please answer all the questions by placing, either a √ or × in the boxes provided.

Course Attended _____

Mode of Attendance ☐   Full-time ☐   Part-time ☐

Day-release ☐   Evening ☐

Age   16–18 ☐   19–24 ☐   25–60 ☐   60+ ☐

Sex   Male ☐   Female ☐

Library Facilities

1 Do you think that the study
facilities in the library are

Adequate ☐

Too crowded ☐

No opinion ☐

2 Do you feel that the amount and
selection of books and audio/visual
equipment available is adequate?

Yes ☐

No ☐

3 How do you think facilities could be improved?

_____

_____

_____

_____

An example
questionnaire.

Activity 7	Working in groups of two or three, choose one of the fast-food outlets in your area and carry out research on who the customers are. In order to do this you will need to decide the sort of information which you want to find out, and then design and administer your questionnaire.

You may find it helpful to read the next section on market segmentation before drawing up your questionnaire.

Market segmentation

This refers to attempts to subdivide the market into a distinct group of customers in order to get a clearer idea of which type of people make up the target market.

For example, it is clear that the consumer market is not made up of a homogeneous mass of consumers; it can be divided up into broad subgroups on the basis of a number of criteria, such as age, geographical location, income, etc. It may be that such subgroups exhibit broad similarities in buying behaviour. People on very high incomes and who are members of socio-economic group A (higher managerial and professional) can be expected to have different 'lifestyles' and therefore different desires and buying priorities from those on low incomes who are members of socio-economic group E, eg pensioners and widows.

The main advantage of market segmentation is that it can improve the effectiveness of marketing operations since marketing efforts are focussed specifically on those groups of consumers who are most likely to want the products offered. There is therefore a reduced risk of wasting marketing effort on groups which are unlikely to purchase the product.

Socio-economic divisions

The table at the top of the next page shows socio-economic divisions. The grading provided in letters is used by the Joint Industry Committee for National Readership Surveys (JICNARS); although not the only classification, it is important because media circulation and viewing figures are broken down in this way.

Registrar General	National Readership Survey	Occupations
I	A	Higher managerial, administrative or professional
II	B	Intermediate managerial, administrative or professional
III(a)	C1	Supervisory, clerical, junior managerial or professional
III(m)	C2	Skilled manual workers
IV	D	Semi-skilled and un-skilled manual workers
V	E	State pensioners, widows, casual or lower grade earners

The marketing mix

The buyers of goods respond to a number of variables when making their purchasing decisions. These variables are termed the **marketing mix**, and include Product, Price, Promotion and Place.

1 Product: all aspects of the product will affect the consumer, including its quality, special features, packing, servicing, warranty and durability.

2 Price: naturally the price will affect consumer demand, also whether credit or discounts are available, and price relative to other goods.

3 Promotion: the level of advertising, merchandising (promotion of the product at its point of purchase) and general publicity will affect consumers' attitudes.

4 Place: channels of distribution chosen, the location and the service offered, will partly determine consumer demand.

We have already examined the product part of the marketing mix in this block, but now need to go on to examine the other elements.

Activity 8 Working in your groups examine the prices of the various fast food outlets which you have been investigating. Can you suggest why the prices are set at the levels you have identified?

Read the next section on pricing to check your ideas.

Pricing

If the market for goods were perfectly competitive with a large number of individual suppliers, then individual firms would have no influence on the price. Price would be determined by the market forces created by competitive pressures and consumer buying patterns, ie by supply and demand.

We have already examined the factors affecting the demand for different products and the relationship of demand to price. We now need to examine supply in order to see how the interaction of supply and demand determines price.

Supply

The supply of a product or service is determined by the ability and willingness of producers to meet the demands of consumers at a variety of prices. If the price which customers are willing to pay is relatively high, then producers are willing to supply more if their production capability will allow them to. As the price consumers are willing to pay falls, then suppliers will be willing to supply less. This is because as prices falls, profit per unit falls and therefore production will become less profitable generally. The relationship between price and quantity supplied can be shown by use of a graph.

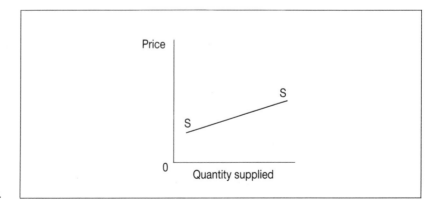

The supply curve.

The supply curve usually slopes upward from left to right, showing that the higher the price, the more suppliers are willing to produce.

Price is obviously the major factor affecting the quantity supplied. However, there are other important factors which can cause a shift in the supply curve. For example, technical progress which may involve improvements in performance of machines or labour, or the quality of raw materials, can result in greater efficiency and a reduction in the cost of production. Such a reduction in costs makes the product more profitable to produce and the supplier may therefore be willing to increase supply.

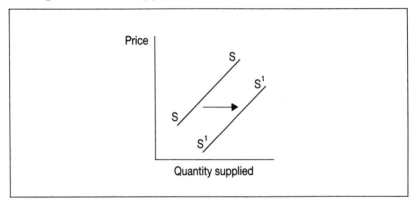

Shift in the
supply curve.

Assume that a car manufacturer introduces robot welding machines onto the production line, therefore reducing manpower costs. Each car made would be more profitable than previously and the producer would be willing to produce more cars at the existing price. This would result in a shift in the supply curve to the right, as indicated in the diagram above.

Another important determinant of changes in the conditions governing supply is changes in the prices of the various factors of production, eg labour, land, buildings, machinery, raw materials, etc. Movements in wages, in the price of materials, fuel and power, the level of rents and rates, will clearly affect the costs of production. The level of profitability of the organization will change and the amount of the product it is willing to supply will also change. For example, if car workers obtain a substantial wage rise, then this will increase a car manufacturer's costs and profitability will fall. Cars are therefore less profitable to produce and the manufacturer will be willing to supply less. The supply shifts to the left as indicated at the top of the following page.

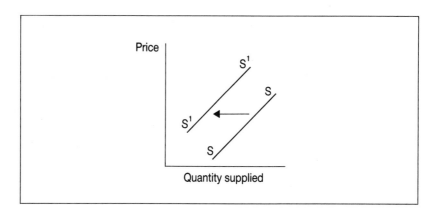

Effect on the
supply curve of
an increase in
price.

Changes in the prices of other commodities may affect the
supply of a product of which the price does not change. For
example, a firm producing plastic garden gnomes could quite
easily produce plastic dolls. If the price of dolls increased,
making their production more profitable in comparison to
the production of garden gnomes, then the organization may
simply transfer productive capacity to plastic dolls.

The Government can, by the use of taxation and subsidies,
influence the production of certain goods and services. The
imposition of tax on a good will tend to discourage
production of that good, whereas the granting of a subsidy
will tend to encourage production.

Supply, demand and price

A market for a product or service is simply the combination
of the supply and demand for it. The point where the market
demand is equal to the market supply gives the **market
price** (or **equilibrium price**).

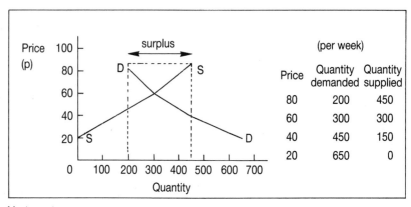

Price	Quantity demanded	Quantity supplied
80	200	450
60	300	300
40	450	150
20	650	0

Market price.

In the situation shown the market price is 60p, for only at this price is the quantity supplied equal to the amount demanded by consumers. At prices higher than the market price, ie 60p, the quantity supplied would be greater than the quantity demanded and the surplus would oblige suppliers to lower their prices to dispose of their output. For example at a price of 80p, the quantity demanded is 200 units but the quantity suppliers are willing to supply is 450 units; there is therefore a surplus of some 250 units.

At prices lower than the market price, eg 40p, the quantity demanded will exceed the quantity supplied, giving rise to a shortage. Competition between buyers to obtain the product will force up the price towards the market price.

Price in a competitive market is therefore determined by the forces of supply and demand.

In most markets, companies do have some control over the price which they charge for their product: price will not simply be determined by the market forces at work.

There are several influences affecting the pricing decision, including costs, competitors' reactions, and the sensitivity of customers to price.

There are several broad approaches to pricing.

Cost-plus pricing

This is probably the most common form of pricing. Firms require a good knowledge of their costs, because to set the price they need to calculate the average cost of the product and then add on a profit margin. The difficulty with this method is that although on the face of it it looks as though, if a profit margin is added to costs, then a loss cannot be made, this may not be the case. An organization's costs are calculated on the basis of a forecasted sales volume, but with little regard for the effect that price can have on demand. Cost-plus pricing may lead to the price being set too high, leading to lower sales than expected and therefore lower revenue.

Contribution pricing

This is a form of cost-based pricing and is based on the fact that two broad categories of cost can be identified. Direct costs are those costs which vary directly with the level of output, eg costs of raw materials, labour, energy. Indirect costs include administrative and selling costs, and the cost of machinery. It is difficult to allocate these costs to individual units of production. 'Contribution' here refers to the difference between the revenue generated by an activity and the direct costs of that activity. It represents therefore the contribution that the activity makes to indirect costs and profit.

The contribution is the surplus which remains after the individual product's direct costs have been subtracted from its revenue. The total contribution of all the products should be sufficient to cover the indirect costs and also allow a reasonable level of profit for the organization.

Marginal cost pricing

The marginal cost of production is the addition to total costs generated by producing one more unit of output. The organization distinguishes between direct costs and those which remain fixed regardless of the level of output. Price is based on the cost of each extra unit of output sold after the fixed overheads have been met. For example the marginal cost of carrying an extra passenger on the railways on busy inter-city routes is much less than that on a suburban branch line where trains normally run with empty carriages. If price were based on marginal cost then the traveller on inter-city lines would pay much less than the traveller on a suburban branch line.

The advantage of this pricing method is that the price of a product can be set purely on direct costs. For example if sales are down, as they will be in offpeak times for hotels, it will be worthwhile offering cheap prices for rooms in order to make some contribution to profit levels.

Competitive pricing

For many business organizations, prices are mainly influenced by competitor's prices. They may not wish to deviate from this price for fear of losing sales or provoking retaliatory action from the other firms with whom they compete.

In a market which is dominated by relatively few producers (*oligopoly*, see page 152), competitive pricing takes the form of price leadership. This arises where one firm, because of its market share, is viewed as the leader and the other firms wait for the price leader to change its price before following suit.

| *Activity 9* | Taking the range of fast-food outlets in your area, examine the advertising and promotion which they carry out. Do they advertise in the local paper? Make use of leaflets and special offers? When you have completed your investigations, read the section which follows. |

The advertising and publicity carried out by an organization are an important part of the marketing mix and are perhaps the most obvious aspects of the marketing effort.

Promotion

Firms spend money on advertising in order to communicate with prospective customers in the market place and to achieve certain results. Perhaps the simplest form is the use of classified advertisements to sell cars; the most complex might perhaps be corporate advertising for a multinational trying generally to create a favourable climate for the firm's operations.

The overwhelming majority of advertising expenditure is directed through the press and television.

| *Activity 10* | Think of as many different advertisements as you can and make a list of the media in which they appeared. Check the range of your list with the section on media below. Try to find out the costs involved in advertising through some of the media you have identified. |

The media

The media provide advertisers with access to prospective purchasers. Before the spread of television, the national newspapers provided the main way of reaching the mass market. There are of course other media available in addition to newspapers, including magazines, periodicals, trade and technical press, radio, cinema, transport advertising and posters.

Award winning
advertisements,
one for a specific
product, another to
create brand
awareness.

The information on total advertising expenditure below
gives some idea of the importance of the various media.

Total advertising expenditure 1984

	£ m
Total press	2558
Television	1245
Poster and transport	150
Radio	86
Cinema	16

Expenditure on press advertising breaks down into:

	£ m
Regional newspapers	921
National newspapers	678
Business and professional	311
Magazines and periodicals	250
Press production costs	216
Directories	182

(*Source*: Advertising Association)

Advertisers use the media for the nonpersonal presentation and promotion of their products/services, because in return they are given access to groups of buyers. The most suitable media will be chosen because of the fit between the profile of their customers and those which the advertiser wants to reach. Consideration will also be given to the cost in comparison with other media. In order to compare the efficiency of different media it may be useful to express the cost as 'cost per thousand'. This means the cost of reaching each thousand of the target audience (homes, housewives, adults, etc). It is usually expressed in pence, and is used as a general yardstick of media cost and efficiency. Cost per thousand can be calculated by dividing, for example, the single-column centimetre rate of a publication by its circulation (number of readers). For example if a newspaper charges £1.50 per single column centimetre (s.c.c.) and has a circulation of 20 000, the cost woud be

$$£1.50 \div 20 = 7.5\text{p per thousand circulation.}$$

The advertising process itself involves three parties: the advertiser who supplies the product or service, the advertising agency which translates the advertiser's need into the appropriate campaign using the best media, and the media owner.

Advertising agencies

Agencies differ enormously in size, structure and the range of services they offer. They carry out work for many clients, developing advertising campaigns which are suitable for each client's needs.

Most large companies, and indeed many smaller ones, will make use of the specialist services of an advertising agency to co-ordinate their advertising and promotion. The link between the advertiser and the agency is the Account Executive who oversees the agency's work on a particular client's account. The majority of agencies offer a full range of creative services, media services and marketing services. Some of the more well-known agencies in the UK include Saatchi and Saatchi, Garland Compton, J. Walter Thompson, and Ogilvy and Mather. An example of the internal structure of an advertising agency is given below:

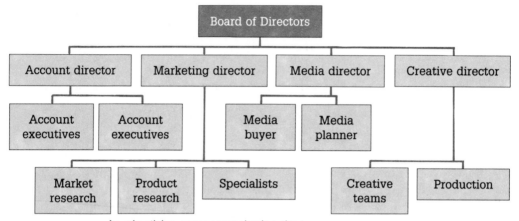

An advertising agency organization chart.

An agency media department will be responsible for the efficient allocation of funds among alternative media. This will include advising on the optimum media for a particular purpose, obtaining the best price, and scheduling the use of the media.

It is the creative department which provides copy visuals, films, scripts, etc, and proposals for innovations and development in both the advertising and the product.

The job of co-ordinating the relationship between the client and the agency and its various departments falls on the account executive, who will also be involved in planning the objectives and strategy of the campaign.

Agencies may also advise on plans for nonmedia or below-the-line-advertising, which is another form of sales promotion.

Below-the-line-advertising

These activities will be carried out in addition to media advertising and can include the following:

1 *Free samples,* often as an introductory promotion. Sometimes the free samples are pushed through letterboxes, or customers are invited to send in to the manufacturer to obtain their free sample.

2 *Free gifts,* sometimes acquired through the collecting of a

number of coupons, packet tops, or trading stamps. They are designed to promote loyalty to a particular product.

3 *Coupon offers,* distributed door to door and through retailers, often providing money off the purchase of specific products.

4 *Competitions,* these vary in complexity and must comply with relevant legislation.

5 *Exhibitions and demonstrations,* eg the Ideal Home Exhibition and the Motor Show, but also including small in-store demonstrations.

6 *Price-cuts,* the normal pattern is for the price-cut to be short-term and for it to be financed by both manufacturer and retailers in an attempt to increase the throughput of a specific line.

Place

The concept of place within the marketing mix is about making goods and services available at the right time, in the correct quantities and at the appropriate place. It covers two broad areas, firstly physical distribution, which is concerned with supplies, stock, storage, transportation and warehousing, and secondly the choice of distribution channels. The way in which manufacturers make their goods available to the market is a fundamental part of marketing strategy. There are a variety of methods available to manufacturers.

Wholesalers have always bought in bulk from manufacturers, usually specializing in a particular trade and selling goods in convenient quantities to retailers within the locality. Profit is earned by the wholesaler by buying in bulk from manufacturers and warehousing the goods until the retailer requires them. The main advantage to a manufacturer of using a wholesaler is a reduction in distribution costs. Without wholesalers, manufacturers would have to make a large number of small deliveries to a wide range of retail outlets.

Supermarkets specialize in the repeat selling of goods for which there is a high regular demand. The operators buy directly from the manufacturer, thus cutting out the wholesaler and therefore being able to offer goods at lower prices.

Department stores carry a wide variety of merchandise with specific departments handling particular groups of goods.

These examples of distribution outlets all involve the manufacturer's using an intermediary. If a manufacturer sells to wholesalers and then on to retailers, the manufacturer will have less control over the distribution and marketing of the product, compared with selling direct to the customer. Also the longer the chain between manufacturers and customers, the less the likelihood of fast and accurate feedback on customer demand and satisfaction.

There are, however, definite advantages to using intermediaries. One obvious one is that the use of such a channel cuts down the number of transactions involving the manufacturer, eg the manufacturer may be selling to fifteen wholesalers rather than one hundred and fifty retailers (who then sell direct to the customer). This may also have the advantage of reducing distribution costs.

The alternative to using intermediaries is for the manufacturer to sell direct to the end–user (the consumer). **Direct marketing** is usually employed by firms selling particular categories of goods, and is often used in the marketing of industrial products. The sales involve high-value dispatches, infrequent purchasing, and the necessity to work to technical specifications, eg the sale of computers. In such cases manufacturers usually employ their own specialist sales force to service their customers.

Of course direct marketing is also employed by manufacturers of consumer products. Examples include the franchising networks already discussed, eg Benetton. Avon Cosmetics employ sales staff to sell to housewives, and many other companies may sell direct from their factories through mail order and catalogues. Manufacturers may also expand into retail outlets in order to ensure control over the distribution of their products.

The nature and complexity of the distribution channels employed by a manufacturer will depend upon the product concerned (its perishability, bulk, frequency of purchase, industrial or consumer nature), who the customers are, and where they are located.

Conclusion

Developing a successful mix of product, price, place and promotion depends upon the match between the marketing activities and the target market. Through your examination of one particular market, that of fast-foods, and an examination of the marketing function, you should now appreciate the importance of marketing to the achievement of an organization's objectives.

Activity 11	Using the information which you have already acquired on the fast-food market and any additional detail which you consider useful, draw up a report which examines in detail the market for fast-food in your locality.

The report is to be used by the small firms unit in your area as part of their detailed reference material available to those thinking of setting up in business.

Summary of skills

The intention of the study involved in this unit is not only to learn facts about organizations, but also to develop skills which will be of use in the business world. This section at the end of each block of work is to indicate the skills areas you should have developed during each activity.

Skills

Skill	*Activities in which skill is developed*
a Working with others	1, 2, 7, 8, 9, 11
b Information gathering	1, 3, 4, 6, 7, 8, 9, 10, 11
c Learning and studying	All activities
d Communicating	1, 3, 4, 7, 8, 9, 11
e Design and visual discrimination	1, 9, 11
f Identifying and tackling problems	7, 9, 11
g Numeracy	8, 11

Links with other units

You should also appreciate the links which exist between your studies in this area and your studies of *People in Organizations* and *Finance*. These activities are related to departmental functions and obtaining and presenting information which you will be concerned with in your work in the *People in Organizations* unit. In the *Finance* unit an examination of financial factors and decision-making will impinge upon the objectives of the marketing department.

Block 9
Case Study: A Firm Wrongfooted by the Pace of Change

Introduction

In this block, the work which you are asked to carry out centres around one particular business. The activities involved draw on, and develop, content and skills from the previous blocks.

The case study involves a firm which manufactures specialist walking and climbing boots and shoes. The firm finds its market share declining and after analysis of the market, the partial answer to its problems appears to lie in the introduction of new technology and changing production processes. You will be required to examine the effects of the changes in production which are suggested and to recommend a course of action for the firm.

Hobsons Boot and Shoe Company
Wrongfooted by the Pace of Change

Situation

Hobsons is a small and well established company. It specializes in the manufacture of custom-made leather shoes and leather walking and climbing boots. The firm serves a fairly small market but is particularly well known for its boots, which are sold to the upper end of the market.

The firm has been located in Northampton for over fifty years but has not changed its manufacturing process a great deal over that time. The firm is labour intensive and has a greater proportion of skilled labour than unskilled.

In recent years there has been growing competition, particularly in the boot market, from European manufacturers. Competitors have been replacing high class hand-made leather boots with equally expensive extruded plastic boots. The Board of Directors of Hobson's realizes that their declining market share in boots is largely responsible for their declining profitability. Analysis of the information given below indicates this.

Market Data	1980	1981	1982	1983	1984
Sales volume (Boots and shoes) (*000s*)	26	25.5	25	24	22
Sales value (Boots and shoes) (*£000s*)	1040	1147	1250	1320	1200
Market Share (%)					
Boots	7.8	7.1	6.6	5.8	4.5
Shoes	5.0	4.8	4.9	5.1	4.9
Net Profit (*£000s*)	120	107	101	93	81

The Board is begining to examine the possibility of also moving into the production of extruded plastic walking boots. The implications of moving from mainly manual methods of production to automated methods should improve the firm's profitability, but it will also have major repercussions for manning levels.

The workforce totals 92 with quite a high proportion of these having worked for the firm for more than five years. The present organizational structure and numbers employed, and the wage and salary structure, are given opposite.

Organizational Structure

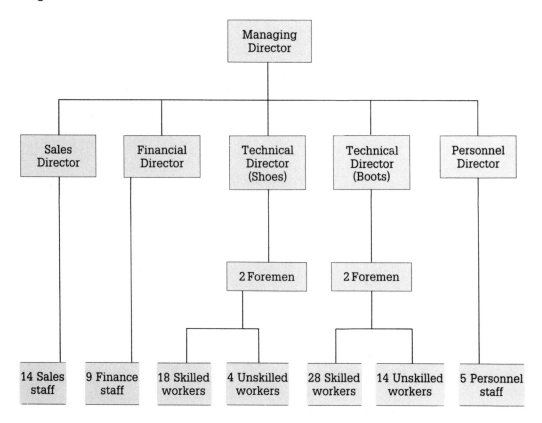

Wages and salary structure

		Average Wage/Salary (£)
Management	Managing Director	22 000
	Sales Director	16 500
	Financial Director	16 500
	Personnel Director	13 200
	Technical Director (Shoes)	17 600
	Technical Director (Boots)	18 700
Supervisory	Foremen	9 350
Clerical and Administrative		6 600
Manual	Skilled	7 700
	Unskilled	6 000

Being an old–established firm, Hobsons has some long–service workers, particularly in the skilled area. The age structure and years of service of both the skilled and unskilled workforce is given below.

Details of skilled workers

Years of service	Age 16–20	21–30	31–40	41–50	51–60	61–65
0–1	1					
2–3	2		3			
4–6		2				
7–10			9	3	3	
11–15			1	7	4	
16–20				3	5	
21+						3

Details of unskilled workers

Years of service	Age 16–20	21–30	31–40	41–50	51–60	61–65
0–1	2	1				
2–3	1	1				
4–6	1	2	2			
7–10		1	1	1		
11–15			1	1	2	
16–20						1
21+						

The clerical and administrative staff at the firm tend to have worked at Hobsons for shorter periods than the rest of the workforce.

Of the fourteen sales staff, ten have worked with the company for less than seven years and range in age from 20 years to 42 years. There are four longer-serving employees within the department, all having worked for Hobsons for longer than fifteen years.

In the finance department, there are four young clerical assistants who have all been employed by the company for less than five years. The other members of the department have between eight and twenty years service. All five of the personnel staff have worked for the company for less than four years.

The market

Faced with declining profitability and a falling market share, the board of directors commissioned a marketing consultant to investigate the market for walking and climbing boots. The results of those investigations and the consultant's recommendations are reproduced in a summary of the marketing consultant's report (see Appendix 1 on page 191).

Production processes

While awaiting the marketing consultant's report, the board also requested more information from the Technical Director (Boots Division) regarding new manufacturing processes. There are clear possibilities of moving from the traditional method of the shoemaker making a pair of shoes from start to finish. New highly automated methods of production may transform the cost of manufacture for the firm.

Details of the new machinery available and some of the manning implications are included with the internal memorandum from the Technical Director (see Appendix 2).

Following the preparation of the marketing consultant's report and the Technical Director's memorandum, rumours have begun to circulate amongst the workforce about possible redundancies.

In order to attempt to allay fears and to maintain a good relationship with the workforce, management and union representatives have agreed to convene a Joint Consultative Committee (JCC) meeting. The committee will discuss the possible effects of introducing an automated manufacturing process.

It is accepted by both management and unions that such a meeting recognizes the rights of employees to be consulted and to discuss matters which will affect them in their employment. The meeting will provide a forum for discussion of alternative courses of action without involving actual negotiations between the trade unions and management. Negotiations regarding matters affecting employment will take place as part of the collective bargaining procedures after consultation. The JCC meeting therefore is essentially a means of exchanging ideas.

Activity 1	Choose one of the roles given below. Bearing in mind the role you have taken, prepare a report which examines the possible effects of introducing the automated manufacturing process and make suitable recommendations.

Role A: Personnel Assistant

You have been requested by the Personnel Director to produce a full report on the implications for the firm of introducing automation into boot manufacture. You understand that the Personnel Director may then make some changes to this report, but it will provide the basis for the discussion of the problems by the management team at the JCC meeting. The items detailed on the Agenda (see Appendix 3) for the JCC should form the basis of your report.

The management team will have to be prepared to discuss the items fully with trade union representatives, and to answer their questions and seek solutions to the problems that will undoubtedly arise if the proposal to automate goes ahead.

Role B: Trade Union Representative

The Regional Official of your union, the Footwear and Allied Crafts Trade Union, is to participate in the JCC meeting, and to advise local trade union representatives on the effects of automation. You have been requested by your regional official to produce a full report of the implications for your members of the introduction of new production processes into boot manufacture. The report will provide the basis for discussion at the JCC meeting by the various trade union representatives. The items detailed on the Agenda (see Appendix 3) for the JCC, should form the basis of your report.

The trade union team will have to be prepared to discuss the items fully with management and to put forward suggestions for protecting the jobs and conditions of any members affected by the proposed changes.

General guidance

In order to deal adequately with the JCC Agenda items, you will need to consider carefully the role which has been allocated to you. Your role will determine the emphasis that you place on, and the attitude which you take to, the implications of the automation plan. It is up to you to analyse the situation of the firm on the basis of the information provided. If you make any assumptions these should be clearly stated.

| Activity 2 |

Depending upon the role which you have chosen in Activity 1, participate in the JCC meeting as a member of the management team or of the trade union team.

In order for the meeting to be evenly balanced it would be best if half your group were trade union representatives and half management. If your group is large, it may be better to organize more than one meeting.

Conduct of the JCC meeting

The meeting should not be overformal; it is essentially a means of exchanging ideas. There are no standing orders to be followed (apart from the order of business) or formal motions to be put. All members should address their comments through the chairperson. You will need to decide who is to take on this specific role. If you wish to reply to another member's comments, then you should make a note of the point and bring it up as part of your contribution when the chairperson asks you to speak. It would be best to make some notes of the points you wish to raise in order to ensure that your comments are relevant and coherent.

The role of the chairperson

To lead the meeting and ensure that order is kept.

Procedure

1 Open the meeting by welcoming members and stating the purpose of the meeting.
2 Explain that all contributions should be made through the chairperson.
3 Deal with items 1 and 2, then move to the main business, item 3.
4 Make a note of those wishing to speak so that you can call them in some sort of order.
5 Try to ensure that all present make some contribution.
6 Try to ensure that the discussion keeps going.
7 When you close the meeting, try to summarize the main points which have been raised.

Appendix 1

Marketing Consultant's Report (Summary)

Terms of reference

To investigate, report and make recommendations on present performance and future market strategy of the boots division of *Hobsons*.

Procedure

1 Analysis of competitors' product strategy in relation to a changing market.

2 Consumer research by individual interview of sample (182) identified climbing/walking boot users.

Findings

1 Undoubtedly other brand leaders, particularly in Italy, have responded more quickly to change in market trends than Hobsons. The history of this changing market probably starts with the industry itself as much as the consumer, and three major factors can be identified:

    a *The search for a less labour-intensive production process*
Traditional boot manufacture is highly labour-intensive and furthermore requires a highly skilled workforce. Rates of production are very slow and are not amenable to much mechanization. These factors have resulted in the manufacturers of high-quality mountaineering boots beginning to price themselves out of the market. This has led to the following two developments.

    b *The development of plastic boot technology*
This derives from the ski boot manufacturing industry where plastic materials and production-line technology have completely ousted the leather, hand-made boot. These techniques are now being successfully applied by several continental manufacturers and at least one English manufacturer producing boots under licence.

    c *Development of the lightweight boot/shoe*
The rapid growth in the training shoe market has created a new generation of shoe technologies. There are now available machines capable of producing quickly and reliably high-quality training shoes. At least two competitors are now producing lightweight boots in synthetic materials using this technology. They have kept the price relatively high in keeping with their brand image, but have successfully sold them by emphasizing their immediate comfort and light weight.

2 *Consumer research*
In the process of this research we identified three major groups of users: Professionals, Enthusiasts, Traditionalists.

    a *Professionals*
Although very small in number, this group is important because they establish trends and fashions which other users follow. Unfortunately for the industry, one of their dominant trends at present is a move towards minimal use of any kind

The marketing consultant's report.

of specialist equipment. This does not apply to Winter or Alpine Mountaineering, where they are nearly all wearing plastic boots.

b *Enthusiasts*

This is the main target group. Our researchers suggest that this is a growing group of possibly 1–3% of the population prepared to spend a considerable amount of time and money pursuing their walking/climbing/mountaineering activities. In social terms they are mainly A, B, C, and are predominantly young and mobile. The ownership of appropriate (and often excessive) technical equipment is very much a part of their style but they are a sophisticated and discriminating market needing careful treatment. Their present concerns are High Technology and lightweight equipment. Price is very often seen to be a secondary consideration.

c *Traditionalists*

In social profile, these are similar to *Enthusiasts* but often a generation older. They are again a discriminating market but much less fickle in brand and product loyalty. In individual interviews the names of *Hobsons* was mentioned many times as the standard by which other firms were judged. 61% of this group already possessed a pair of boots made by *Hobsons* and another 10% said they would like to own some if they could afford it. Unfortunately they saw the purchase of these boots as almost a once-in-a-lifetime activity and saw no reason to repeat the purchase in the near future.

Conclusions

1 The market for high quality climbing and mountaineering boots is bouyant and expanding.

2 Product quality, brand name and current fashion are more central factors in the decision to buy than price.

3 New technology boots, both plastic and trainer style, are being heavily marketed by several major competitors with considerable success.

Recommendations

1 The traditional style and manufacturing of high quality leather climbing boots is certainly a declining market except amongst older customers who do not buy frequently enough to sustain a viable manufacturing process. We estimate this area of demand, plus a small export market to the US and Canada, at about a steady 6000–8000 pairs per year.

Apart from this very small area we recommend that *Hobsons* discontinues the production of leather boots.

Bearing in mind the market image of the company of high class, specialist reliability, we further recommend that the process is switched entirely to high-quality plastic mountaineering boots. This product is now of proven quality and with considerable sales and export potential. The training shoe type boot is still of uncertain quality and we would suggest that other companies are left to speculate in this area until both product quality and potential market stabilize.

Appendix

We attach examples from the trade press reviewing recent new footwear.

A NEW SOLE

Conservation is a factor that most backpackers and walkers are concerned with, to a greater or lesser degree, and with more and more people apparently taking to the hills and footpaths each year it is undisputed that erosion, caused by many pairs of tramping boots, will occur.

I looked at this very problem in some depth a few issues ago, and put forward some thoughts on boot construction that I thought might help the situation. It has been my belief for some time that most walkers and backpackers are "overbooted": heavy mountaineering boots are worn when something a lot lighter would be both easier on feet and terrain, and I am convinced that much damage is done to hill tracks and footpaths, and in certain situations, to vegetation, by the harsh cutting effect of modern boot soles.

Ken Ledward of Klets, a man whose involvement with the outdoors goes much further than just testing gear, has been in regular contact with me since that article appeared. ("Tread Softly", Climber and Rambler, Jan. 1979.) Unknown to me at the time, Ken had been working on the design of a boot sole which would have less cutting effect than the average lug sole; an ecological boot. Ecology apart, there were other reasons for Ken's interest in this field.

In early 1977, Ken decided to make a determined effort to study the performance of outdoor education students, using a variety of footwear; gym shoes, running shoes, orienteering shoes, walking boots and rigid climbing boots. From this survey, it was discovered, that apart from certain circumstances like rock climbing, wet weather and winter conditions, all preferred to use the gym shoe, or some form of training shoe. It seemed that most people wanted a comfortable, lightweight type of footwear for general mountain use. Ken also noticed that those wearing the lighter footwear tended to move faster in the hills, had more agility, and suffered little problem with blisters or sore feet.

Armed with the findings of his observations, and from test results taken from all areas of Britain, Alpine Europe, the U.S.A. and Canada and East Africa, Ken began considering alternatives to the standard patterns.

Tom Waghorn reviews new gear for the Eighties at the Camping Trade Exhibition

Step Out Lightly . . .
A LIGHTWEIGHT revolution is hitting the outdoor market—a revolution which should see lighter and more "ecological" footwear on the feet of the ever-growing multitudes on Britain's hills.

Ultra lightweight boots were pioneered by Winit a year ago and now comes the first of Karrimor's British-designed summer sports boots and shoes which are aimed mainly at the booming hill-running, mountain marathon and jogging brigade.

The soles are the idea of Ken Ledward, the pint-sized gear-testing enthusiast who pounds the hills of Lakeland from his home in the Duddon Valley in the cause of bettering the equipment you use.

One of the ideas behind the soles is that they do not pick up earth and small stones. Result: less wear and tear on the hills.

This is particularly important in the eighties as anyone who has viewed the appalling erosion on the Lyke Wake Walk, Pennine Way, Snowdon and parts of Yorkshire's Three Peaks will confirm.

And the astonishing explosion of competitive hill-bashing from the Karrimor Marathon to the Ben Nevis Race has brought a demand for a better-quality, purpose-designed fell-running shoe.

Although the new footwear has a British concept, design and development, it is being made in Italy by Asolo, one of the world's leading manufacturers for mountain feet, and will be known as Asolo-K-SBs. Karrimor and Asolo have done a deal on marketing and distribution which will ensure world-wide availability.

Why not "made in Britain"? I understand that there were

snags with prospective British manufacturers and that Karrimor managing director Mike Parsons was determined to "get it right" before this month's launch. So Italy it had to be. Britain couldn't provide quickness, quality, efficiency and the right price.

Appendix 2

Hobsons Boot and Shoe Company

From   J. Mellish   To   E. Dunn

      Technical Director (Boots Division)   Managing Director

---

<u>Subject</u>   Plastic Boot Manufacturing Procedures

Further to your request for more information regarding new boot manufacturing

processes, I am now in a position to submit a summary of my findings.

I would also like to put on record my considerable misgivings about this

proposed change in manufacturing processes. This company has always been

admired for the quality of its workmanship and its good industrial relations

and I believe there is always a market for the best. In my opinion these

plastic boots are a passing fad and demand will soon swing back to the

traditional hand-made boot.

<u>Summary of Technical Director's Report</u>

The availability of plastic boot technology.

1 It is suggested that the initial production target for plastic boots

    should be 18 000 pairs per year.

2 <u>Equipment</u> There are only two machines available which will produce

    high quality plastic boots; one is Italian and one Japanese. There

    is a two-year waiting list on the Italian model. The Japanese models

    cost approximately £95 000 each and at least three would be required to

    meet the production target. They could be delivered in three months.

3 Operation

    a <u>Shiftwork</u> To make effective use of these machines it would be

       necessary to work some sort of shift system. The manufacturers

       recommend they should run for between 120-140 hours a week for

       maximum efficiency. Longer than this causes increased frequency of breakdowns. A shorter period than this does not permit sufficient return on capital.

b <u>Manning levels</u> Each machine would require three operatives per shift to service and feed it. Since the process is semi-automatic, these three operatives would produce completed pairs of boots from raw materials without any further assistance. Each shift would also require a foreman/supervisor and some sort of manning allowance for personal time of the operatives.

c <u>Training</u> Training of one man per machine comes as part of the purchase price. Training of further personnel to use these machines will cost £60.00 per operative and take three days. If we were to choose the three original trainees carefully, they would be able to train the other operatives themselves.

Appendix 3

Hobsons Boot and Shoe Company

JCC MEETING

The next meeting of the Joint Consultative Committee will be at 10.00 a.m. Friday 24 April 1986 in the Board room.

AGENDA

1 Minutes

2 Matters arising

3 Proposed automation

        - manning levels

        - cost savings/implications

        - profitability

4 Any other business

Index